OBLIVION

OBLIVION

POEMS BY

STEPHEN BERG

University of Illinois Press
Urbana and Chicago

Publication of this book was supported by grants from the
National Endowment for the Arts and the
Illinois Arts Council, a state agency.

Manufactured in the United States of America
P   5   4   3   2   1

This book is printed on acid-free paper.

Portions of "Sappho: You Burn Me" first appeared in
TriQuarterly. Portions of "Rimbaud" first appeared in
The Kenyon Review. A limited edition of "Bankei: First Song: 1653"
was published by Harry Duncan at the Cummington Press, Omaha,
Nebraska, 1990. "Cold Cash" first appeared in The Kenyon Review.
"To My Son" first appeared in The New Yorker.
Portions of "Oblivion" first appeared in Countermeasures, Denver
Quarterly, Ploughshares, and Passages North.

Design: Cynthia Krupat
Cover painting: Sidney Goodman

Library of Congress Cataloging-in-Publication Data
Berg, Stephen.
Oblivion : poems / by Stephen Berg.
p.   cm.
ISBN 0–252–06457–7 (pbk.)
I. Title.
PS3552.E7025   1995
811'.54—dc20   94–24516
CIP

To Toshiko Takaezu

But for those obstinate questionings
Of sense and outward things,
Fallings from us, vanishings
—WORDSWORTH, *Ode:*
Intimations of Immortality from
Recollections of Early Childhood

•

Thus when the bodies are combined the surface does not
exist, but has perished; and when they are divided,
surfaces exist which did not exist before. (The
indivisible point is of course never divided into
two.) And if they are generated and destroyed, from
what are they generated? It is very much the same with
"the present moment" in time. This too cannot be
generated and destroyed; but nevertheless it seems
always to be different, not being substance.
—ARISTOTLE, *Metaphysics,* III

CONTENTS

1 / SAPPHO: YOU BURN ME

        you burn me   burn me burn me

                          these arms can't touch the sky
whose   his   yours   do you love him
                               two minds   better

            to me

                                          wind   heart of a little child

            fantasy

                              •

there is   the problem of the night
            touch   O who   and I yearn for you

who cannot touch the sky   well   one day I saw
                                         the prettiest girl
                                         picking flowers
            there is   the problem   of
                                                 of   dawn

                              •

        sleep next to me   fingertips graze my face

                          the bright and beautiful belong

            what a thought   to the desire of the sunlight

3

nothing destroys

gold   moth worm   neither can eat it

not one human heart has ever resisted it

or the moon

•

stay   where

dawn shifts   like the lyre

•

sheep goats   everything's in blossom

blinding me   like gold like these moist virginal thighs

who can   who will   in the darkness between

•

I have you now naked stretched out on new cushions   here

my hands my tongue   shaken

no bees no honey   talk with me

pain   stories   the one who can weave them

together

sucks in the sweet air between us

my hard nipples and wet   somebody who

                      blames me   let the same frenzy
     break him   conscious
                        delicate hem grazing my feet   whiter than an egg

                              •

air   words   each gorgeous star is lost
                    sipping   like speech
        when we lie touching   when the full moon
                        drowns everything   the way you drown my heart

                              •

I wanted you here   fire   blessing   distance again
                  I know

                              •

            cricket cricket   songs from your wings
                        delicious high-pitched
        sun   everything's
     and   what I need is

night

                eyes closed   like a

   child

                                  clinging to its

mother

•

                one long drink of wine
                because of my pain

•

with what eyes   look me in the face   forgotten dead
               you burn me

•

this is Timas   dust   taken into the black earth unwed

              all her friends took knives
              and shaved off their hair

and Pelagon   dust   his father has hung an oar a fishing basket
                    to praise his hard life

                              •

this gold cup with knobs like knucklebones halfway down
                              o moon moon   time
                    never stops   I'm alone

                              •

            can't act can't move caught in this rage of love
                        where nothing is

                              •

            consciousness is
                                    you love   me like a god
                        these tatters of my voice the wind tears at
                    tongue-tied
death can have me

                              poor   in an instant
                                        scorched ice

trembling breathless   who are we   pulse like the sea

·

blue evening star
        bring sheep goats   the child home to her mother

·

                but this bird   reminder of spring
                such tiny feet   dance at the altar
                trampling the fresh grass   wealth worth
        friends in a dream   whistling

·

I could say what I remember about you is
                purple handkerchief   gift
giver
                                a wildness crushing
                ingenuous

I prayed our night would be two nights

moonlight filtering through your gown   two
                                radiant nipples   and the
dark sweet
                        triangle

                                •

kings and daughters and the daylight making us all
                        beautiful   immortal

                                                song

                                •

                        adolescent hands
                        tearing off yellow flowers
                        my fiery moisture

                                •

            honey   bees   none
                        and death
                        with or without you

I need you   come   Sappho needs you   the air's angry
                    with oblivion

                                        •

here we are young women all night at this door singing about love
bride bridegroom when dawn comes and you leave may Hermes
lead your feet with great kindness with the luck you found asleep
her breasts as sweet as violets

                                        •

        sing make me free of beauty   so close to each other
                        like yesterday
                                    when   you sang
at my house   to me   a road where   we   should
always

                                        •

predict nothing   but o   vines   conduit
            your eyes pour into me   what what
        feeling   the rush

the Gods hate death
if not they would die

•

and I'm already dead
or why would I   is this the deep shame often
why would I   my love's   insatiable
haunted by terror

•

listen   my stubborn heart
won't give it to you
ever
so

•

there is
this
seeing I see things   gods passions
my arms   legs   my whole body
stars flung on the sky

                    because forever nobody will ever
                    touch me   dust
        o touch me now   kiss these eyelids breasts thighs

                              weeds
the moon   right there above your shoulder

                              •

              how I ended how my
                                        voice
                                            pottery
                  shards   other men's voices

                              •

                  no girl who sees the sunlight

will ever sing like you

                              •

                              myrrh
        softer than fine linen
                        not you   to me
wish   how long   awkward child
        even then   I loved you

pain

        you give it   about

        with one of your stories   about what

                •

chaos   O the dark texts the spaces

                •

                        stars in an
    unknown order   could it be this voice trying to return

        my heart and your heart touch
        I can feel how we
        will always shine back
        fair face upon fair face

        deeper than flesh and blood

                •

    doves when they sleep grow light
                    pinions
    unintentionally

wings
        invisible

and I'll leave behind
of the muses   foam
                                        conscious of this

                                        •

rich goat fat flares on the spit   bubbles
                                        Aphrodite
                                                        for you
and dawn and the sick frenzy I wish on anyone
                                                who
                        blames me

                                        •

                        Brocheo
sitting watching your face   I can barely breathe
        what are you   I a god like this   given your voice
                        given your soft laughter
I can barely speak

                        Brocheo who are you
veiled eyes there's a singing trembling sweat trickles from every pore
        nothing's left I'm pale green grass to my soul   poor

        delicate fire and death and a dark burning
                                there   my death

apple branches   chattering in the breeze   high up one
untouchable
                              brookwater
leaves   someone asleep

•

not you   not you

•

            half of me   half of me
I can't move   split   here

•

quiet   listen to yourself   it's anger

•

           wet knotted linen

if you felt love if you spoke the truth instead of filth shame
wouldn't cloud your eyes

                              you would ask me for it right now

                    •

             Peace irritates me   especially now
          anise woven in her light-filled hair

such little feet   this altar

               what flute   where   in which world are
we

                    •

             time again   time   threshold as always
                              o mind
          dream   and in it a sign   Hermes   I told Hermes
             I wanted to die

                    •

             something I played on   I hold
             like a small child's tongue

one star beyond all   though it utters nothing
                    though it cannot be touched

    Hesperus   burns me

       and what I leave for you is

            •

gold-wreathed Aphrodite I wish I could have it have it have it what
       is it   about the word mine about mine

            •

invisible   humming to herself   to me
       somewhere

          does not come to my bed

            •

   immortal Aphrodite   throned gold   listen
                           fly down to me

on the dark earth   who shall I strike with love whose heart
shall I break   drawn to me   fleeing me

       come now as you did once   soothe me

  war

Cleis   yellow exquisite

flower   daughter   they offered Lydia   Lesbos
for you

            I said No

                •

      dawn enters step by step   everywhere

death   festivals
bowls cups people arriving   old women men singing
      and always in my mortal heart your heart death

                •

not you who are   to me   who what
        gods
          flute lyre   through this through every word
touch
     what we do together
            worship
                  which is what

take me   when nothing's left

                                        •

                              headband   exile   memorials
exhausted   the beach at twilight
                                                            bowls chalices tipped over
                  on the misty beach

                                        •

O master   Hermes   take me below   clear dew
          I see my death   and the other shore
                                        me you   and

                                        •

                    the feeling is   I can't have anything again   ever
            except
                              calling   who   nobody's clear voices
who   in me

some say men on horses   some say men on foot   some report men on
ships   but I say it's what you love   Helen left everything   I

     remember
               Anactoria   a thousand miles away
   her face would change in an instant   it shone   it made men on
horses
       or on foot   nothing   like the nothing of this distance
            that kills me

•

   and no   holy no   man   was
there
                       no grove
     memories   wishes   always

•

    Gongyla   I wanted you but you

          would never
though I held my mouth
        Gongyla   never
         for days   ideas of death flit

sapling   o the green

        standing in the bright air   marry her

•

   love has shaken me

                 like wind rushing down from the hills
hitting a grove

     of oaks
you burn me
with what eyes look me in the face

                        friend to friend

nothing's sweeter than sleeping with your love
      it heals the dying soul

with what eyes
        what pain love gives
you burn me   show me   what's behind your

               eyes

       a breeze now   what is

2 / RIMBAUD

THE IMPOSSIBLE

(for Lou Asekoff)

Rain, snow, icestorms, peaceful sunny days, I was riveted to life, a beggar cruising the endless road. Oblivious, stupid, proud, preternaturally calm, who needed friends or country?

O my ecstatic childhood, I was right to hate what I hated. Listen: in Hell we don't give even the dying a penny, but we're civil. We see the world correctly. We're not salesmen. Nothing hurts us, not even the surly, confident ones, the false elect, who humiliate us, refuse to bless us.

Western swamps, you've sponged up all the light! My soul won't stop grieving. I'd have to strangle myself to end these bleak hymns honestly.

When I confronted the King of Hell, I said: Fuck martyrdom, fuck the sublime glow of art, the seriousness of inventors, the fervor of businessmen and thieves. The East is a dream of never waking up. I wasn't pondering my escape from contemporary anguish. I wasn't exploring the spooky Koran. Ever since Science took over, Man hides from himself. We cultivate fog, eat fever with our watery carrots and broccoli. We get drunk, smoke, sacrifice ourselves. Infinitely distant from the root, we exterminate ourselves with our own poisons.

Rabbis and priests, this is not Eden. Time doesn't exist. The world has no age. Formulate your own East, older than the stars. Don't give in. You're free to live beyond suicidal schemes of salvation. Science is much too slow for men like us. Cherished Western citizens, wake up. Your souls are asleep. You're still addicted to the human. Truth's everywhere, as close as our own hands. Weeping angels hover close to us. Soul, soul,

this pure, radiant instant—sinister turning of ten windmills by the edge of a bare field in a black and hungry year—crucifies us.

Human work—eyes, hands, fingers, toes, groins squeezed against metal! Necessity, grenade after silent grenade, explodes in distant corners of my abyss, whenever it wants to.

Work is much too slow. What can I do? Turn prayer into a wild horse! Let light thunder! I see it, it's so simple, so clear—hotter than a furnace door. You won't need me when you see it too.

Pity me—my life is like a cheap torn coat. Reality cries fuck and eat everything, desecrate the world's masks: politician, beggar, poet, slimy administrator . . . priest! When I was in the hospital—what was it?—wisps of the stink millions of people left behind in confession boxes, a kind of acrid, sacred residue in homage to our tragedy, suffocated me, exposed the sleazy education I got as a child. So what? I can reach twenty, if you can.

Listen, you bastards—I refuse to die. Work is trivial, my pride won't tolerate its chain of empty minutes.

Priceless fragile soul, are we cut off from eternity forever? Would that teach us to be free?

Oh now I can hear Mankind lifting its hopeful voice: "Vanity doesn't exist! Science is salvation! Move your asses!" while the corpses of parasites and convicts freeze the hearts of humble men like us. Beyond night itself, beyond even the most remote planetary edge of the future, God waits to redeem us, and we can't shun that blinding fate.

HAPPINESS

Each of us is doomed to be happy, forced to live many lives. Each of us will be crushed on the anvil of terror, reborn by awe. Action isn't life, it spoils God's power, it drains the last prayers from our throats. The soul's theater is invisible—sight, hearing, taste, smell, senses without organs.

Listen: each of us lives many lives—plumbers, angels, athletes, electricians, gods. Once I was a pig. I champion all axioms of madness. I lived them all, I know the system.

Terror gnaws my mind. The same dream drags me back into it, destroys the real world, calls me to inhabit it permanently. I'm ready to die, ready to be wind, darkness, ghosts.

God's final curse is a live coal broiling my tongue. Islands and blue sea, I dream you'll wash away this disease of unspecified truths, I see the cross loom like redemption. The rainbow led me here, where remorse gnaws like a tapeworm dragging itself out past my lips. My life is immense, I won't dedicate myself to muscle and rhyme.

Deadly sweet tooth of bliss, aria—in the gloomiest cities, at dawn, you warn me. I hear you first in the gossip of the men who raped my mouth and ass. Then in windswept leaves. Two truths. One truth. That's the final terror we all have to accept—not one or the other, but both, like a friend's face whose torn-out eyes still recognize you.

The tiny bud scared me. Vicious landscape. I did everything to escape it. I told people I could visit them inside me, mocked the current darlings of poetry. Their courteous bows to the smug audience of approval made me puke.

Porno magazines, rotting Victorian travel books, medieval passion plays, junked movie sets, refrains from old songs, languages I couldn't read, musty albums packed with snapshots of the family desperately trying to smile—through all of it I saw that hard young body begging to be loved.

I even invented a religion without icons or rites. I wrote a brief manual of prayers and regulations, I established walking and sleeping as the two basic forms of sacrifice. I described God: obese, lazy, dressed like a stockbroker in His pink shirt and chalk-striped flannel suit, puffing on a cigar.

I invented vowel colors, reshaped the cadence of consonants, consigned each syllable to a branch on the elm outside my house. I deleted the senses from poetry until all I could hear was a faint abstract whisper like the breathing of a horse thirty feet away. English! English! My precise identity babbled its proofs in dreams.

Nothing worked. I wrote silence. I wrote night. On scraps of wrapping paper, I scratched down hopeless love. I paced my crummy room like a squirrel—significant, hyper-acute, pathologically quick—

but she would not be erased, a thousand years younger by then, spread-eagle across my mind, inches from my face, the gash between her legs, its ethereal brown hair and wild node, a crown I licked all over until she came.

The blood of black Neanderthals fuels my veins. Holy spirit, you're near. Why doesn't Christ help me? The Gospel's garbage on the street in front of a whorehouse.

I wait for God like a man watching all his money in stocks plummet. Cell by cell, I'm doomed, I'll never rise above these roots.

I stand on a western beach. Let houselights, streetlights flare when evening comes. My days on earth are finished. West, your salt sea air sears my lungs, islands and weird empires burn my skin. I want to bathe in those waters, trample grass, hunt, smoke, get drunk on booze as strong as boiling metal, crouched like my ancestors at the fringes of campfires.

When I come home my arms will be iron, skin like a starless night, eyes like a tiger's. Pouches of gold will dangle from my waist, I'll be idle, brutal. People will fear me. Politics will save me. I'll lose myself in politics. Women will offer me their naked breasts and hot cunts.

I hate this country. I was born exiled. How else can I become God, how else can His silent invisible clarity occur? I'm going to drink this whole bottle, right now, sleep on the sand, and dream a world-shaking theory I can't prove: The mystery of God is the mystery of one's own identity . . . etc.

Rimbaud. civilization handcuffs you. These aphoristic gunshots aren't poetry. You're so fucked-up no technique can shape your despair. I heard whoever I am speak, I followed him, repeated words, exchanged their meanings, hallucinated chemical shifts—a rose into a tree, a living room under a lake, long black roads jammed with carriages in the sky, a school of drummer boys conducted by an angel, babies' heads on old bodies— I alchemized my heart into a black stone. Music of words stripped of meaning, exposition to deify lyricism, formulas like "God is, by definition, without dimension . . ." became eschatological proofs. I prayed the melodrama of my lost faith would raze cities, bark not sing, reverse existence.

My personal chaos became a makeshift religion. I started that fad in society. I was the one! Sweet animals, caterpillars drugged by their innocent limbo, arrogant moles, smooth deep sleep of virgins! I wanted to be anyone but me—whoever that was. I wanted to be the one understandable word on a tablet in a cryptic tongue.

Finally I stared into the mirror until the boy in the glass and the boy outside were one, then smeared the word GOD on it with a shitty forefinger.

I'm not bored. No rage, faggotry, madness—I'm relaxed now. Clear your minds, consider my innocence. I'm not asking for pity. I don't want to marry Christ's daughter. Listen: I'm not limited by my rational mind. I told God I want death. That's the one freedom. These days I'm concentrating only on what's essential. No frivolous tidbits, no devotion, no need of divine love. No sadness over the age of my sensitive heart. Each of us has reason, scorn, gratitude. Let me take my place on top of the angelic ladder of common sense.

Familiar happiness? It's not for me. I'm too dissolute, too weak. Life thrives through toil—numb platitude! My life isn't heavy enough, it flies and floats high above action, that precious focus of the world.

God, give me celestial airy calm, reverence, sainthood, change me into an angel whose work sings God instantly into men's flesh, blood, marrow. Nobody wants that anymore. What a perpetual farce. What a naive idiot I am. I'm practically an old maid. I don't have the balls to love death,

obsessed with that great image of mine, oh, that sick psalm—one lone fly drunk in a hotel toilet, crazy with excrement, cooked by a random shaft of sunlight!

PAIN

The rich can't sleep. Wealth should be everyone's. All the rich know is lineages, but I've had to transcend my own suicidal habits, my own mute gift for oblivion. Now I'm good. Nothing to repent. But the clock still strikes the hour of absolute pain. Will I end up like a child, in Paradise, without sorrow?

Divine love's the only key to knowledge. Nature's a display of pure goodness. I'm through with demons.

The rational song of angels teaches salvation: Divine Love. I'll die of worship, of loving the bare earth—both! I condemn anyone my departure would destroy. Save my friends, save the shipwrecked passengers!

This ground under my feet is good. Sane at last, I'll bless life, love my brothers. No more childish promises. No hope of escaping old age and death. My strength is God. Praise God! His omnipotent abstract transparent hands soothe my face.

No early death for me—sons of good families, coffins glistening with crystal tears. I've been rescued by the white man, converted, baptized, dressed in work clothes, chained to a job. What a relief! Christianity's blade, stuck straight through my heart.

Even as a child the incurable convict gorged me with awe, all those doors closing behind him, that chorus of iron. Blue skies, fields bursting with wild asters—I knew they were his idea of himself, his bleak, particular fate. He alone witnessed his own glory. Reasonable mind, tenacious as a saint, more practical than a traveler, a seeker everywhere, nothing could tear his image out of my head.

Winter nights on an empty road, naked, without bread, a voice froze my heart: "Weak or strong, it's you: pointlessly walking, go in anywhere, say anything to anyone, they won't kill you, you're already a corpse. That's your strength."

Suddenly the black and red mud of cities was a mirror, a lamp carried back and forth in a locked room, winking under the door, a gold shield in a forest. Good luck, I yelled. A sea of smoke and flames, all the wealth in the world, flashed like a billion thunderbolts, looted the sky!

A screaming mob caught me. Blindfolded, propped up in front of a firing squad, I wept out of pity for the evil they could not grasp, and forgave them. "Priests, professors, misers, merchants, generals, my white masters, I'm from a race that sings under torture. A brute, a black beast whose eyes can't see your courteous light. I can't be saved. Let the law kill me. I have no morality, this is a mistake!"

Do I know nature yet, do I know myself? Not one more syllable. I'm digging a grave in my belly for the dead. Howls, drumming, delirious savage dances.

HANDS

Beggars are too honest, they disgust me. Blue-white my eyes, skull narrow as a broom closet. I'm like the Gauls, I don't butter my hair. With the splended disdain of kings, I love all the vices.

Bosses and workers, slaves, the hand that writes with the pen guides the plough. History is hands! Will I never possess my hands, be cared for by invisible gods, fed by the sky, entertained by water? Devious tongue. I'm lazier than a toad. Feeble, Christian notes, lovesong, what was I in the last century?

You geniuses at profit and loss, what is the body? Do you recognize your body? Progress is a great god with a mouth and no asshole. The cosmos is a mechanical toy. Chemistry in a teaspoon. The world moves forward, an army without shoes.

The revelation of fate in numbers is clear. I can't explain what I mean. I'm not a ditchdigger, I don't fix wagons or doors. Driven toward the Soul, like hungry cattle, I heard sounds without reference to things outside themselves—the poor a clashing Hell of symbols. Your demolished silence, a king with no mouth.

SEEDS

Inside this wailing skin, I'm still alive. Shirt of flame, remember Paradise! Purged of all human hope, like a huge cat, I mutilated joy's face, chewed on my executioners' wings. Disaster was my God, I groveled in mud, dried myself off in the breezes of crime. I acted crazier than myself. Spring's idiotic laughter crushed my heart.

I dined at the sacred feast that gave me back my appetite. Infant soul, I knew the tiniest gesture of your finger, lip or eyelid was a rite of mercy, a suicidal plea.

Why look back at the old roads again? Drugs and buggery flourished. My grief took root. Why inspect each vice that started when thought dawned? It wounds the sky, drags me into the black future.

This is the last innocence, the last introverted peek into the reamed-out precincts of Hell, the last choral swoon. It's over—betrayals, disgusts, my effigies of a metaphysical unknown.

Who wants to hire me? What beast should I adore? What face of the divine defile? Whose hearts should I break? What lies should I defend? What blood should I wade through?

Avoid the police. Live poor. With a withered fist lift the coffin lids, sit until you evaporate. *Mon ami*, terror isn't French.

I'm so alone nothing about me rises above the paltry earth.

My punishment? To take one step after another, lungs frozen, head a blast furnace, my daylight eyes drenched with night.

Time duplicates us after death. Where? Will we really be the same?

Shoot me in the face or I'll jam this pistol into my raving mouth, jump under those wheels. . . . Oh, I welcome it.

Fire in my guts, dose of holy poison crippling me, I'm a live corpse almost reborn, but I slipped away. Happy, good, I'm ready for salvation, and yet Hell won't tolerate my song of insolent hope.

Life grinds us into ash. My parents baptized me, that watery bliss enslaved me, slaughtered me with ardor.

Hell, bless me! Only fresh crime could plunge me into nothingness. Give me Justice, Her scales emptied of the past.

Childhood comes back: grass, rain, the lake over stones, moonlight oozing through the roof of the belfry when the bell struck midnight. Fatal ignorance, nursery rhymes, Mary, Virgin Mary, you're a lie! Don't touch me. I smell like roasted skin.

This is truth— There's no history. Wealthier than a king, I decode secret wisdoms, postulate the immortality of tables and chairs.

Life's clock stopped hours ago. Theology is somewhere else. Straddling a green wave, Jesus walks on purple thistles, Jesus walks on stormiest water. This ecstatic sleep of mine unveils the mysteries.

Have faith, follow me, pathetic, exhausted laborers, fragile children— astonishing human heart!

Hell, I'm sold on your glory, your worms and pitchforks, holocaust of lust— I've decided to be reborn and study every maimed piece of myself, kissed by Mother Earth. God, hide me, hold me; these words, sniffing the ground, are starved dogs pocked with sores.

I'm hidden and absolutely clear.

Smear dress shop mirrors with wet dirt, choke lovers in bed with powdered rubies—change me. I live and live and live.

Lost. Drunk. Filthy. But listen. Forgive me. Down here. Friends. No friends. Raped by ghosts. Insane. Damned and dead. But grieving, terrified.

Testicles. Breasts. No city. I follow her. No choice. Punished, but I follow. Not a woman or man.

Reinvent love, whippings, blood, grovelings, that voice, like death itself, a little girl, singing, grieving without words.

No mind. A sleeping body. Watched. Outside, thinking. Dreams? Dangers? The key? Slaves of compassion, despair, we protected each other. We knew the world was here.

Angel in her soul. Sorrow. Two children trapped in a Paradise of sorrow.

Sick with the terror of leaving, can anyone hear God? Shame of the sleepwalker.

I know: some day at the same moment we'll both disappear.

I was young. A hero. They wrote my story in gold, my frantic tale of Hell. Real Hell. White-hot doors that open. Christ's hands and feet.

Eyes fixed on the silver star, my pain blinded me. I was the first one to sing the song of people under a fair sky.

Autumn. Infinite sun. Beyond the changing seasons, our tiny boat, fire, mud, wet bread. Love's crucified mind, love's actual gazes and touches.

Heart riddled with worms, cold earth, identify these strangers. Am I dead?

At times I see endless beaches of white nations, cured by raptures of joy. I lead festivals, victories, tragedies. I invent new flowers, new stars, new flesh, new speech.

Every pore of my feet kisses the ground. One task: to love reality like a peasant.

Am I wrong? Are death and charity twin sisters?

Forgive my lies.

No hands, no help.

Everything's clear! Don't move. Dried blood smokes on my face.

BEAUTY

Last night, I sat Beauty on my knees, kissed her, sniffed her sour breath, cursed Justice, thrashed Hope out of my brain, gave up Religion, despised anything I could name, butchered Joy. I saw my rose of tenderness shriveled by fear. I saw myself as a child when all hearts opened, all wines flowed, and I wanted to die.

But, in a great dream, I thought: Find the key to your life. And it appeared: Charity.

I shook black from the blackish night sky. I became a spark of raw golden light, a clown, a blank-faced clown, so carefree all I did was smile. My mind was like the sky on one of those mild bright late April days you wish would last forever. Not one cloud floated by. Consciousness was outside me, asking, "What are you going through?"

Is the idea of God enough, can it console you?

"Rimbaud" is my response to various English translations of Rimbaud's *Une Saison en Enfer.*

3 / THREE POEMS

BANKEI: FIRST SONG: 1653

never was   always will be
mind before mind
earth water fire wind
sleep there tonight

you you on fire
burning yourself
attached
to this burning house

search
all the way back
to the womb
can't remember a thing

good bad
ideas
self self
which?

winter's wonderful
bonfire's
ridiculous
in summer

summer breezes
irritate
even before autumn's
over

rich now
you hate the poor
forget when you
had nothing

you saved every dollar
a fiend
watched by famished wraiths
of your self

your whole life
making money
could not pay off
death

clinging wanting
nothing on my mind
that's why I can say
it's all mine

you want someone you loved
now
only because
you never knew her

you can't forget
not to remember
someone you never forgot
who?

looking back
you see it one brief evening
realize   see
everything's a lie

bitter? does this
incredible world of grief hurt?
why wound yourself
brooding on dreams?

all this
is unreal
instead of clutching your head
go and sing

no hands   no eyes
nothing exists
touch see
that's it

your mind
yours
torments you
because you need it

hating hell
loving heaven
torture yourself
in this joyous world

the hating mind
itself is not bad
not not hating
what's bad

good   bad
crumple into a ball
of trash
for the gutter

ideas about
what you *should* do
never existed
III

finished
with Buddhism
nothing's
new

enlightenment   really?
"mind"
keep wrestling with yourself
idiot

these days enlightenment
means nothing to me
so I wake up
feeling fine

tired of praying
for salvation   look
those poor beautiful flowers
withering

saunter
along the river
breathe
in   out

die   live
day and night   here
listen   the world's
your hand

Buddhas
are pitiful
all dressed up   dazzled
by brocade robes

enemies
come from your mind
right wrong right wrong
never were

call it this   that
it doesn't exist
except this page
except these wandering phrases

praised   abused
like a block of wood straight through
my head's the universe
can't hide my ugliness my clumsiness

so I just go along
with what is
without anger
without happiness

nothing to see   nothing to know
before after now
call and you'll hear
its heartbreaking silence

Peter Haskell's translation of Bankei's "Song of Original Mind," published in his *Bankei Zen* (Grove Press, 1984), formed the basis of "First Song." I read his version endlessly—tired, irritable, helpless, listening to my mother ramble one afternoon in the aftermath of a serious yearlong illness, for the greed of my baffled ear, I found myself beginning this vastly different poem. Much later the last three stanzas came, inspired by other pieces from the same wonderful book.

the way is hard   choose choose
don't like or dislike   everything's clear
one hair between them   earth sky
not for not against   the truth is clear
for and against   mind's worst disease
no rest   deep meaning not understood
blank featureless space   just enough
taking rejecting   we think it isn't so
getting entangled   as if it's real
driving away pain   pretending it's unreal
pain vanishes   serene in the One
stop moving to rest   rest will be restless
linger on either   the One is lost
without the One   you're lost forever
get rid of Reality   sink deeper into the Real
clinging to the void   denies what it is
talk about it think about it   it's far away
not liking exhausts you   feuds do nothing
following the One   don't hate the senses
accept the senses   perception is true
the wise do least   folly shackles itself
why prefer anything   why be attached
why thought and thought   who led you there?
ignorance is rest unrest   no love no hate
dream ghost flower in the air   why try to hold it?
is isn't gain loss   bury them forever
eyes open in sleep   can't have bad dreams
not this or that   nothing but truth
the mysterious One   dissolves memories
think of the One   is is is is
no beginning anywhere   no battles left
movement is still   then where is it?
stillness moves   then where is it?
both gone forever   where is the One?

at the final point   with nothing beyond
no rules   all standards gone
all's equal   action is action
doubt's washed away   belief is easy
nothing left over   nothing remembered
don't speak don't think   everything's known
return to the root   the meaning's there
seek the light   you'll lose its source
look into yourself   in a flash
what seems what is the nothing of it all   is yours
don't look for truth   give up your views
is isn't   breed chaos madness
the two exist because of the One   forget the One
no thought   no blame
no blame no truths   no nothing no thoughts
who does what he does   vanishes
nothing is done   when he's gone
who does what he does   does it
space is bright all by itself   no mind does it
no one understands   that amazing sphere
beyond yet here   neither he nor I
The Not Two   is the best term
nothing apart   everything here
this truth was   before all
forever and never   are the same
see it or not   it's everywhere
to trust in the heart   is The Not Two
The Not Two   to trust in the heart
and my serious words   mist
these things   that have no
yesterday   today   tomorrow

DAITO'S MIND

look
truth's naked radiant flesh
the core shines by itself
no eyes no ears

sky's like a sheet of pure aluminum

nothing
no words for it
desperate to find me
nothing you see

air's fragrant as an elephant fart

or hear
is where I am
point to it
just like that

wet grass as tender as a baby's heart

without texts
you are it
just like that
try to see me

road's empty not a car man or dog on it

through form through sound
in either place
you can't see me
so many years begging

trees leafless like the bones of thought

robe's old torn
outside the gates miles of grass
sleeve tatter
chases the moon

hunched on my rainy stoop the old neighborhood cat

roaming everywhere
no footprints of mine are seen
on one tip of a hair I leave the capitol
three drum taps I leave Kyushu

car coughs two three times can't start

one glance at the morning star the snow got even whiter
the look in his eye chills hair and bones
if earth itself hadn't known this instant
old Shakyamuni would never have appeared

sink your teeth into this juicy arm

how boring to sit lazily on the floor
not meditating not breaking through
look! horses racing along the Kamo River
that's zazen!

falling asleep's waking to your first face

scoop up water
the moon lies in your hands
toy with a flower
its fragrance soaks your robe

one day I'll lift myself for the last time

please drink this cup of wine
beyond the western outpost
you'll find
no friends

nothing but walls of mist miles ahead of you

full moon in the palace pond a gem
though it's not yet autumn
this very quiet night he's sure the ripples are different
from this alone he'll walk the path deluded

wrought iron garden chairs like black skeletons

as if he had new eyes
huge Dantaloka Mountain hard as iron
cold windless night
but bamboo whispers

a world trying to know itself speak in unison

I push away from the lamplight
the scroll of half-read texts
only my mind listening
not one master left

this right hand fist can't bang the sky's aluminum

mind slices a hair
blown against it nothing is cut it cuts itself
nowhere everywhere happens I hear
the emptiness gnash its teeth

taste its black mouth

4 / MYTH & OTHERS

O howls of crystal, milky souvenirs, desire piercing its own unsleeping
    eyeball with desire, glimpse of the ephemeral soul, bed where we
    talk and unfold and confess the impossibility of autobiography,

What else is there to our lives except your head raging with snakes and
    echoing skies, walls brushed gold by centuries of light, leisures of
    pure design, dreams of a relaxed god who serves and saves and
    provides whatever next wish blossoms into the faceless smile of
    mortality.

O birth of an endless self, imagine us without you, poor scavenging
    guests condemned to work, poor burgeoning weeds singing like poets
    without words,

Possibly value, possibly the last murder, possibly gray, possibly
    nothing less than a blind fuck in an alley, possibly tradition and
    belief, possibly even the wild god of hope inspiring the suicide of
    wishes, preventing our failure.

But imagine someone dying and you wake up and 18 million is yours, left
    by this unknown uncle from Davenport, Iowa, and there you are in the
    real world for once, not art, the world of having and owning and
    never having to die, of being better than, above, the world of
    gilded snot and full-fed lips and sleep unbroken by loss, pigskin,
    peach silk cushions, cupolas, Louis XIV Roman chairs, the clear
    sweet light of complacency flowing in from Sardinia.

Who knows what it would mean, the central Chinese figure for this might
    be some wizened bald guy in robes sitting on a cushion chanting
    while I hum to myself "As Time Goes By," who knows what we really
    hope to achieve when one of those stark moments of truth
    overtakes us and we feel absolutely free, calm, happy even, and can
    choose anything instead of being held in suspense by all we know we
    can have,

Which is nothing according to Medusa's wailing mouth in the statue I
	saw reproduced in House & Garden, and tore out, and study right now
	as I am writing, thick gray slit of a mouth, huge voluptuous lips,
	blank eyes, a residue of carving where the pupils were chiseled in
	relief, and of course snakes for hair.

And yet we think of love, and the failures and the relentless calling
	to us we hear from its pale villas and graves, war heroes, that's
	what lovers are, I can see us, the deepest glance into the soul, the
	gaze not even a high Mexican valley can equal.

The point is what can money do but remind our vulnerability to
	act and awaken to itself and become the new shield which
	the army of nature with its loving unknown deaths may pierce and
	restore our souls to the laughter of revolving doors taking us from
	the inside weather of a lobby to the outside street of lighted
	buildings, skies, gusts of intense stupidity and fun.

So I was told by my real mother, whom I cannot remember, what could be
	crazier than to marry oneself but that's what money is, a broken egg
	at the bottom of a torn pocket, a tabletop in which we see our
	hungry faces, but there isn't a dish of anything on it for us to
	eat.

Very funny, someone cackles inside, I was only five when someone handed me
	a book with ten red white and blue stamps in it which would someday
	become a bond which would someday become cash if I bought more
	stamps and waited long enough, what was wrong with me? I just found
	that very book in my dead mother's panty drawer, (I was collecting
	her things), I guess I never cashed it in.

That's me, in my never-ending attempt to be a husband, not to mention
    son, father, fisherman, gardener, runner, great lover, just a normal
    American citizen, not Mayakovsky, not a guy who believes he can face
    death without a tear or a little shit in his pants,

And yet among these helpless ruminations there's another thing—what
    does the earth want from us, if anything? what are we supposed to do
    for the sake of it all as emissaries to an unknown kingdom?

I thought this was funny once, but not now, not even the weirdness of
    Mallarmé or a pheasant dinner can distract me from asking how and
    why it was done, instead of answering by picking out a Jaguar,
    Baum et Mercier, or a beachfront condo to console my enviable loins.

O even my own ordinary tables and chairs are laughing at me for having
    them so close, so deep in my mind that when I come home nights I
    almost greet them with a word of praise and relief—who belongs to
    whom?—what a rich question, since no more stories of the past are
    possible, on this yacht of material possibility.

Sometimes in the bathroom I'll be standing there cock naked loving
    every minute of it, maybe even liking that place and time better
    than anything, the cozy steam of the hot water turned on full, the
    mirror clouding up, readying myself with a shave, then
    adjusting the shower water just right for the day so I can step in
    under the stream and not decide how long to take, feel I have hours,
    then begin to regret the necessary exit I'll be making before long
    into the dry commercial world of dog-eat-dog, of schedules and
    tasks, of making success better than that opposite term, which is,
    after all, the nature of the universe.

But will we ever know it, will the shower ever be our home? on certain
days a feeling overtakes me, sits like a happy dog in my belly, of
being poor, of having nothing but friends and poetry and a warm
place to sleep, and it occurs to me that intelligence of this sort
is denied to those who cannot hear the crystal howling or see the
milky souvenirs or experience the despair of desire's baleful stare
or know the soul's unyielding misery as it lies back letting its
voice unfold the nonfactual snakes of light, of a destitute prompt
unmotherly hammer driving in the nail, in the dirty unpainted wall
of truth is beauty, beauty is truth, you know it and it's enough,

O which is why Let me touch you, Touch me, lie like two transparent
knives willing to be picked up inside each of us, for no particular
use, on no table, in no man's silver sheath, sparkling as the light
at any time plays through their blades in the eternally joyful
hands, ridiculous as Tolstoi, that cannot pick them up.

TO MY SON

In the car, bitterly yearning for a kind woman
I hadn't seen in years, I turned to the driver—
"I'm leaving, I'm leaving. Let me out, now!"
But first, I asked where my son was,
and he jumped up from the floor, perched on top of my fist,
a white mouse I bent my lips to and kissed
and held against my cheek.
The car sped on. There was a feeling in this dream,
just before he appeared, of grief, and I
can't recall—something, something.
My wife was at the wheel. We battled. Rain.
Trees, blacktop, hillside seen through a blurred windshield.
A line I wrote in my sleep is lost too,
its cold plain words, like these, worthless terms of meaning.
What happened before the scene in the rain-drenched car
is me straddling a woman in bed, biting
very very gently through sheer white silk
her nipples, then cut to the road, wife, mouse,
anguish. Whose voice or face keeps signaling,
crying out from a great distance in the mind,
from a life I know I should live? The sweet
poor beast that came when I needed my son . . .

TALKING

When I sat with you, listening to you
talk about your life, some ageless sexual reaching out,
odor from deeper than I knew, went through me—
I wanted to touch you,
unbutton the button you kept fingering on your blouse
as if your left hand were trying to begin a story
while your voice wove through divorce, war,
friendship, medicine, poetry.

In England, when you were a child,
your mother read Dickens to the family
each night, acting the characters, but in Oaxaca at 90
she can't see, she bends her face to the pages, missing words,
uses a lighted magnifying glass you gave her.
I peered into the jungle there once
and saw, or thought I saw, Indians flickering between
the green vines and trunks of their world and mine
in the dry, white streets,
like your voice, moving between us.

In the reddish, barroom light,
you declared your love for Chekhov:
"If there is an afterlife, where we meet,
he is the first person I'll look for."
His stern, friendly, amused voice seemed to be there with us
in the dark booth, cracking jokes,
teaching the first lesson, if we are to live and write—
"compassion to the tips of our fingers"—

and I could hear
that passage in *Gooseberries* where Ivan laments happiness,
where he says none of us
sees or hears those who suffer—
nobody cries out, their silence keeps us happy—

where he says someone with a hammer should knock on our doors
to wake us until other people's pain becomes ours.
But there is "no man with a hammer."

On a scoured, tarred oasis of bulldozed ground,
trees tilted in earthfilled burlap sacks
lashed to their roots
as they wait
on the lips of their fresh holes,
under fifty bare floors of an unfinished high-rise
a block from home, years later—
clouds, birds, the life of the sky, black bits
flashing across its uninhabited glass face—

laughter seizes
the air between us.
I hear your voice.
A strong gust brings it to me.

WINDOW

I was sitting in my office today,
window open, smoking a cigar,
and saw steam from an invisible chimney
reflected in a skyscraper window—

two huge gray panes
letting vapor play
across their bright faces,
one shape swirling into another;

even while the sun thinned or got brighter
those clouds kept squirming across,
and even might have risen on the inside,
but all I knew—knew the instant a chill

rushed through me like a truth I hide from myself
and say No! to and therefore know is true—was
that screen of forms yearning through space to the infinite unknown
        Other we can't believe in
is the soul, and felt safe.

SURF

Death's close, each instant's utterly itself,
no before and after,
just still being here amazes me,
just knowing I'll be gone soon stuns me.
I dream of loving and killing,
women undress, approach, comfort me tenderly
by whispering crude kind sex words
nights when I wake, can't sleep,
fantasize sweet skin, wet lips, blue famished eyes.
God knows what life would have been
if I had married so-and-so, left Philly,
saved money, played the market.
On days like these my soul's drenched by a fine rain,
swathed in desolate silence; heroes
ghost the vanishing battlefield of my brain.
Hemingway's bullfight book includes a shot of him at fifty,
trim, muscular, genitals bulging through wet trunks,
his giant calves half-sunk in Spanish surf. White
close-cropped beard. White foam and sky.
Hands down, palms white too, spread open toward me,
white teeth, he grins, unaccountably happy,
eager to greet
whoever sees the page,
planted forever at that point
in the mute sea,
twin white wakes sucked back against his legs as it ebbs out.

STICKS

Despair was what I called
what drove me into my yard
to prove my love of nature, to clean up
winter debris—sticks mostly.
If I pushed my nose near leaves, if I bent down
astonished by detail: veins, cracks and lucent pools
trapped in the folds of rock, green stems, moss clumped on bricks,
first leaves the size of a baby's fingernail
popping out of every branch I came on
maybe I'd live forever.
A Little Sally Raisin Creme Pie wrapper
had caught in the leaf tangle
of grapevines planted between us and our neighbor,
its dirty cellophane
note from no one to nobody nowhere.
That usually happens when I go out to commune.
I'll be hoping for the cosmic philosophical
and what I'll get is a fuck symbol—
a smiling teen piece in a short skirt,
cunt whiffs of wet earth, moist
shiny bushes that have flourished overnight.
But I gathered leaves, stray
foam nuggets used to pad things in shipping,
plus, fallen dead from the trees, various sticks
which I clipped and made into two neat piles.
In the chilly morning sun
their twin forms
glowed with Oriental mystery.
By that time I had worked up a hard-on
and held Little Sally's mouth on it for at least an hour
until, back inside, all I had to do
was lift her perfect body on to me.

RITUAL

We sat on metal card chairs. Green plastic rugs hid dirt workers had
    flung up when they dug the hole.
A stranger handed me the bronze box, which we passed between us,
    held in our laps, shook,
four of us
listening to the bone chunks, swish of ash.
I stepped down, left it in the hole, stepped out.

Late May, out of the Little Schuylkill, a trout hit
as I glimpsed the purple splash of a flower on the opposite bank,
jerked my rod, hooked it, played it, lifted it, thrashing, into my right
    hand,
inched over to the bank, smashed its head against a rock, and saw that
    night
in the grilled moist meat and fine bones

wisps of her face.

CHERRIES

(for Jeff)

In late April, cherry blossoms engulf the front of the house,
bright bursts, lascivious branches stroking the windows and walls.
Briefly the petals intensify, soften then fall, and the pavement
next morning is hidden by a dense pink sheet.
I wish I had a mind that could penetrate . . . what? The stubborn
sense of something unrevealed, which might be merely these rooms,
their meals and walls and floors,
their prosaic themes of unstated longing?
At the restaurant last night my old friend, Jeff,
was afraid he wouldn't eat in time to drive back to the suburbs and see
        his wife and daughters, so he left.
His wife had finally forced him to move out, and two years later,
dating a new woman, he needed to be in two places at once.
He couldn't simply not be near his wife.
We were sipping wine, talking, watching faces, feeling at home, yet I
        needed to be
in two places, too, or . . . what is the feeling?
There were sea bass, pompano, trout, displayed on ice,
three snug rows facing us on the counter where we sat
waiting for a table.
They had a freshness I envied, they looked innocent,
their scales and harmlessness, sleek oval shapes and motionless poise,
        empty eyes, locked mouths, calm.
"Is my understanding only blindness to my own lack of understanding?"
But there is no understanding today, only yearning . . . for what?
The tree is stripped; its translucent leaves tint the air,
our entire pavement and front steps glutted with petals.
My friend calls to tell me
he finds no solace because his wife still haunts him, it's a curse,
he can't live if he doesn't have her,
and I say we all have a version of this,
this anguished, nameless precinct of the mind, where
we only partly live, this . . .

We call the petals beautiful, miraculous, a gift, as if they marked the
        path to that "something," just out of reach,
but aren't they so truly what we are it's a threat—
soft, faded, blown off when the time comes, trampled, beyond desire?

When he told me about the breakup of his marriage, about his wife fucking other men now, (that's what he believed), that he wanted to die because she wouldn't take him back,

Then, a year later, about being caught in the parking lot minutes after he squeezed the metal and wood office chair into the trunk of his Honda Prelude,

About not understanding why he stole it, why, even after he knew security guards were watching, he continued to fit the chair into his trunk,

When the chair became the main theme of his suicidal shame, his helplessness, his endless daily calls, I felt some clue to the secret of his cure had been revealed, though I had no idea what it was.

He needed to be forgiven, redeemed, but for what, after all? Surely not for something as common as divorce, surely not for stealing a cheap chair from the addiction clinic he ran.

I try to see him in the parking lot, lugging the worthless object to his car, setting it down, unlocking the trunk, wrestling it in until he saw he couldn't close it, jumping into the car, and a guard appears and asks what he's doing.

"All I wanted, really, was to sit down, to rest . . ." I hear him say, and it's crazy, it makes no sense—chairs are everywhere. Why steal a rickety old chair from your employer?

Poor friend, what could have soothed your infinite need? Last night, in a dream, bearded, disheveled, drained, exactly as you were, you sat so close your breath and hair smelled real, you were hoping for a word, and I yelled, "Go away! You're dead."

The guard's hand thrust through the car window, grabbing your shoulder, the transfixed menacing glare of glass and painted metal through the windshield at that instant, wild with detail. . . .

But you can't describe the event, its textures and traits, shapes, gestures, light. You can only sketch auras of mood. Jeff, I'd ask you, and you'd be silent. You thought your confusion meant you had no right to speak. You believed words betrayed you, even in your poems where you grieve for an unnamed woman, for your soul infected with the silent wish to die, with the necessary theft of the chair. You equated silence with truth. I'd sit with you, day after day, helpless in your silence.

Two years after your wife demands you leave, hours after you slave all weekend to start a Japanese garden behind your new house, your heart stops, then the monthlong coma before the tubes are pulled and you dissolve.

Sit in it, feel it under you, relax; stand next to it, place your hand on its backrest; kneel, rest your head on its seat. Cool green steel legs, rivets, laminated wood.

The chair is an afterimage, a thing smoldering in the air.

Your final silence hums on the air.

December. Gray sun. Bamboo seedlings, grass, sky. Squatting to a rock that weighs much more than you do, your face crammed against it, you stretch your arms and hands around it; for the hundredth time, try to lift it, lean, kneel, clutch it tighter, squash your cheek and chest against it, grunt, jam your fingers under it, half-stand, push, hold your breath. Your life is like the darkness inside the rock, inside your brain.

The chair is a blindness that will kill you.

WRITTEN ON A BLANK PAGE IN SCHWERNER'S *SEAWEED*

"catastrophe
love
roots

the ordinary in eternity
and in time
conflict between language
and vision—at a certain point
in his life a man may decide
to keep his vision whole by
disregarding the restrictions of
language while he knows the price this guarantees—
failure, failure that can be
experienced directly by the reader
for the failure's not hidden
behind the false perfections of
form or behind the poet's
need to retreat into
'successful' ways of compromising
his vision by reducing it for the sake of 'beauty,' 'coherence,' 'reason'"

What was I trying to explain?
Why is everything I write not what I wanted to write?
Is love the catastrophe whose roots can't be known?

Which reminds me of a dream:
Infinitely gentle space, a house, no walls, no hills, infinite.
My grandmother's near, I'm dragging in a dog, its crippled forepaw
curls under, it limps on three legs. I beg her to let me bring it in
and she says Of course, Steve, her kind warm tone a solace, a kiss
that lingers long after the dream.
I want to feel I'm inside the word 'room.'
I kiss the dog's yellow head and smell it and hug it to my face.
Isn't there any embrace or thought that can stop this?

Some dreams feel like shameful darkness is being hammered into smears
     of sinister hidden images.
I slip a condom over my head—which head?—and feel the long steel of
     my penis yearn for its twin of wetness.
The dog is inside. The scrim of the dream is ripped off, leaving less than
     the world began with, a pure white void, a nipple.
A zone lurks behind the void, where seer and seen fuse into the trance of
     space between, and I'm in it.
My mother on her deathbed in coma kept mumbling, "Where's my
     mother?"
in the voice of a terrified girl.

ORIGINAL FACE

It must have been the five-hundredth time I sat facing him
in his black leather chair about ten feet away, a window on my left
overlooking the parkway, green lawns, cars, the museum, sky,
unraveling dreams, doubting, dissecting my life
in a voice at times that sounded like a stranger's,
piecing it together detail by detail while I looked away, looked back,
stared at the floor or wall, examined his face
as if I'd find it there.
Sadness in the air between us:

Weiner (analyst) pokes his fist in my face—
"There, at last . . ." opens his jacket,
shows me a shoulder holster, big pistol in it,
whips it out, jams it into my mouth.
I stand my ground, in the dream, anxious.

Nose dream (large knowledge): picking nose.
Analyst: You have Large Knowledge. Great, if only I knew what it was.
An intrusion to my mother. Rest of the session is silence.
Large nostrils. Picking my nose in front of her. I'm an intrusion.

A naked black man brandishing his glossy long black prick
in the streets roves near me—I watch, and whisper, 'Be careful,'
(everywhere a tone, melody, ambience of soul
I can't name that might clarify the dream's core).

Faith? In what, in whom? What's marriage? Money?
What is the "will of God"? Is acceptance God's will?
"Uncertain certainty"? Forgetting? Not killing oneself?
Laughter in the sessions, insights, a flux of selves? Purgatory?

"It may be wondered what state is welcome if desires and memories
are not. A term that would express approximately what I mean to express
is 'faith'—faith that there is an ultimate reality and truth—
the unknown, unknowable, 'formless infinite.' The analyst has to
become infinite by the suspension of memory, desire, understanding."

one by one five people appear each is a silent koan
standing in front of me each one's dissolved solved
simply by looking into its mortal anonymous eyes
a cloak or figured cloth swaddling a prince
lies at my feet lift off the cloth no prince look up
a square opaque gold window glows on the wall
some ancient silver seal
shaped like a fingernail
fixed dead center

The room had pale green walls, paint flaking,
a flimsy standing blackboard, fluorescent fixtures, deskchairs,
a drafting table at the front for the teacher.
The class was big, about thirty, and met nights at 7
and because the course was Autobiographical Fiction
(Sophocles, Conrad, Proust, Melville, I forget who else)
always the feeling that we shouldn't speak,
always the ache of the texts reminding us of ourselves.
Week after week I tried to teach the books,
theorize, analyze, ask questions, but the students rarely spoke.
I'd dredge up remnants of my life to inspire the monologue,
becoming, I felt, an autobiographical fiction myself.
One night we were on Oedipus:
"Man after man after man / what are we" then "nothingness" then the
        moment O. learns who he is,
stabs his eyes out, hears the chorus call all men Oedipus
no matter how lucky, rich, blessed by a god,
kneels, embraces his two small daughters, grieves for their existence,
urges them to "live now, live for today," and is led away.
Then I remembered weeks before
I had visited a Zen master,
still afraid of losing myself, of being known,
still a child questioning his lost mother,
anxious to hear words that would break through
his baffled, cornered mind—I
wanted us to use things he said like "Cut the root!"
and "one has to grasp the world from the side of nothingness"
to fuck the myth of disguised consciousness,
to eat her silent body, sheer shadow now,
mind vs. mind breaking against itself,
my interpretive chalk phrases on the board
tangled in fainter ones from classes before.

Each ribbon of fire seeking love darts quivers in pitiful roses
      gives birth to the burial of the day before—I don't know if
      the drumroll where I look for it will be in clutching a rock or
      the endless birth of the heart

A grave plumb-line stretches in hypersensitive axis toward the
      depth of beings—Destiny's thread! love will deflect that law
      of life toward the voice of man we'll be free in blue trans-
      substantiation we'll be virtuous against the blind and fatal

Within every pure zero isolated in fragile dawns may the
      superior Jesus from another great Beginning throb! And then one
      other line—a Baptist who watches watches watches and rides an
      intangible curve with one foot bathed in purple

"Life is forever turning toward a man
an infinitely vacant, discouraging, hopeless, blank side
on which nothing is written . . ." or
". . . I always think that the best way to know God
is to love many things . . . one must love with a lofty
and serious intimate sympathy, with strength, with intelligence,
and one must always try to know deeper, better and more.
That leads to God, that leads to unwavering faith . . ." or
". . . I think that if one keeps one's serenity and good spirits,
the mood in which one is acts as a great help." Of course. Oh yes. Yes.
Please, Vincent, say more: "You talk of the emptiness you feel
        everywhere . . ."
he wrote Theo—to help, to prove God exists,
to say to his brother: We must see Him, touch Him, believe
that His great wisdom made trees, bridges, fields, skies, ears, crows—or
". . . a splash of black in a sunny landscape . . ."

"A caged bird in spring knows quite well that he might serve some end;
he feels well enough that there is something for him to do,
but he cannot do it . . ." "One cannot always tell what it is
that keeps us shut in, confines us, seems to bury us, but still
one feels certain barriers, certain gates, certain walls . . ." "Do you know
        what frees one from this captivity? It is very deep serious affection.
        Being friends, being brothers, love, that is what opens
the prison by supreme power, by some magic force. But without this
one remains in prison." Please, Vincent, say more:
"What am I in the eyes of most people? . . . a disagreeable man . . . the
lowest of the low. Very well . . . then I should want to show
by my work what there is in the heart of such an eccentric man,
of such a nobody" ". . . a Robinson Crusoe or anchorite . . . otherwise
        one has no root in oneself, and one must never let the fire go out of
one's soul, but keep it burning."
Oh yes. Yes. What color is the soul?
". . . a splash of black in a sunny landscape . . ."?
". . . the mysterious brightness of a pale star in the infinite"?

STOLEN PHOTO

Who was that boy sitting cross-legged on gray grass
in shorts and tank top, hands folded in his lap?
Behind him, a field full of miniature parents,
strolling, visiting their kids at camp.
He leans toward the lens, restraining a faint scowl.
His dark hair's the same shade as the grass.
His ears stick out from his head. His arms are thin.
Slipped between pages of an old novel,
he carried it at 60 in his book bag for a while,
amazed it was him, unable to recognize the face.
Also, he wanted to show it to a woman he knew.
Recently, at his analyst's, he left the bag
on the waiting room table during the session.
Who could be looking at it now, who
would they see, posing for his father? A rag
of cloud's caught passing above everyone,
a cement birdbath tilts near his head, threatening to tip over—
maybe they laugh at this tanned unknown
middle-class camper's annoyance, or fury,
not knowing how he got there or what or why
or whether it's someone's son now or if he's dead,
that is, if they even found it.
The last time I examined it
a speck was breeding in the upper right-hand corner
like decay or the shapeless innocent shape of a soul.

When a voice said "Turn it" that's what I did—turn pain into pleasure, sex into the mad asceticism of the saints, eating into starving, faith into the desolate loss of everything I've always needed, always loved. Then I stood there in bikini underpants squeezing my face in the mirror, making ape grimaces, flexing my arms, admiring the thick white hair on my chest, posing like an athlete so I wouldn't think of myself as a short, helpless Jew. I found along the mirror's edge areas of rotted silver—I could see through to a fragment of wall, or recall the erratic withering of flower petals or imagine the window to a second world where nothing needs to see itself before it dies the way we do. I pressed against the sink, leaned forward, studied every pore of the glass's decay, forgot my face and body. Then "Turn it" came again, and I took the gilt-framed antique mirror in both hands, lifted it down a few inches onto the sink and turned it around. The wire it had hung from was frayed, there were dim scrawls in what looked like a child's handwriting—"hidden myself here" "who never speaks" "who cannot die" "pity" "whose face is the" "except this" "with Go (faded) unfor (faded)" "leave un (faded)"—plus, on the dry cracked brown paper backing, three water stains shaped like a woman's kisses, lips open.

BURNING

(for Rickey Wagman)

Neighbors had made a garden out of a small lot on the corner and were digging furrows, planting seeds, nailing up stakes and chicken wire, the barbershop was there, its short plump owner dozed as usual in one of his two leather and porcelain chairs, his old TV churned its flimsy images, the Russian Orthodox church was closed except for the wing where the homeless lived, dropped my letters in the mailbox near Black and Decker across from the juvenile detention center and 9th district station, passed the hot dog and pretzel man by the library, strolled around Logan Square's Calder fountain by the Museum of Natural History, the huge bronze breasts and thighs of the goddesses gleaming water, Four Seasons, limos, Cigna, up 18th to Rittenhouse, it was all there as before, and why not, sweat started on my palms and forehead when I realized This is all there is, it began and it will end, they say, This is all there is, it is burning, birth death like a palace of leaves, burning, saw dogshit clog my cleated sole scraped it off on a curb then on grass by a tree, then used a twig, the hundred different quartz watches, buttons, displays, black and silver, in the electronics shop across from Pour Vous, Sue's Fruits and Vegetables with its packed stalls juice machine customers, Rindelaub's restaurant now nothing but a cheap bakery, even the faeces, even, Christ, even the cracked fucked-up pavement under my feet, the gift of its drab heart (pray? should I pray?) burning—these must have told me what I had always known in my prideful terrors, but I can't say, only God who needs no God can, or insects communicating their next move, or the pulse of a leaf—every building, shopper, car and garbage can was erupting with the praise and grace of existence, a kind of delirious grief in gratitude for the possibility of existence, *who* yearning for *who* yearning for *who*, it was weird—instantly I resisted, window-shopped, studied books skirts shoes, watched faces, did my interminable shit-scared cretin philosophy, calculated by the feel of bills in my pocket if I had enough for lunch, any appointments?—but it was happening: picture yourself caused by light witnessed by light stated by the throat of light redeemed by light

BLUE HERON

(for Warren and Jane Rohrer)

I was sitting on the long screen porch behind the house in Vermont over-looking the big field fringed by birch and pine when I saw my first heron skim the trees, cross the field in front of me, and land on the far edge of the pond. It backpaddled its wings to slow as it landed and, gently, like a helicopter, eased itself onto the grass bordering a stretch of reeds. Then it waited, snapped its austere oval head sideways, aligned with the water, as if it wanted to listen to rather than see what might be alive there. Or could it see clearly only out of a single eye? Its style of action, a calm series of pauses fused into an unimpeded rite, so voluptuously slow, is how water obeys, unconsciously, wherever it is. Then, surgically, miraculously, it stepped through the water at a speed calculated not to break the surface. You would not say it moved as each twig of a leg sank: the bird strode the steep narrow bank, fitting its weight, its bare physical life, with impossible precision, to the place itself. The pond was impassive dull green. Late August. Less than an hour before twilight. Haze hung in wisps. Yellow and red dashes among the trees. It stopped. It peered down or seemed to meditate in the midst of some cryptic occupation, poised on one leg, the other raised a bit, bent like a debutante's wrist. Then it started again, aiming its gray beak here, there, its gestures issuing from an interior far far from me among the galaxies of an alien mind. Its enormous grace was not an attribute of the human, although oldsters doing Tai Chi resemble this creature's indivisible presence. It reached a boulder and shot its beak into reeds and shadows along a section of rock that jutted over the water. It sipped bugs off the greenest stems. Then, quite nonchalantly, its beak stabbed the water—a blink—without making the least dimple, and I thought I saw a glimmer as it flinched its irregular S of a neck and stretched it straight up at the sky. Occasionally the surface got bitten from underneath, then ripples. The heron continued to stalk, listening; for minutes it did nothing but hold significant, odd postures, all silence, an unbreathing statue. Watching it, was I there, immersed in its state of divested self-corporeality? It always "knew" where it was and what to do. It was my paradigm of concentration. Its hypnosis of self-possession seized me, and as long as it stayed I was a disciple of this process of immaculate balance performing its innate, sublime harmonies. After maybe an hour of no apparent success at fishing, it slapped its wide wings down against the ground and hauled itself, preposterously, without momentum, like some too-old body, up from the realm it had investigated for a meal, and sailed into the dark pink nowhere back across the field.

MYTH

Behind everything—windows, doors, walls—like a dim face,
the myth of a better life exists, but it seems like death
beckoning, trying to wreck what you've worked years to build.
You feel it will kill you when, in fact,
it may be the life you were meant to live and haven't.
All these years living the wrong life. Is it possible?
You've been good—your ass pinned to the chair to write:
poems, letters, checks to pay bills—
so good yet so instinctively punished by hands you finally see are yours,
    miraculous old fingers
with their three bitten nails, long blunt piano fingers.
Now you're sixty. Now you are driven to decide.
Now you've been resurrected by the absolute silence of God.
Now you can't flee time's lesson—that the end
is here now while each puny syllable appears
like notes heard by a blind man, sung by a beggar in the street.
It's like stepping into a dark room before the eyes adjust—
things almost exist, space almost exists, you almost exist.
But a fresh inkling of love, a star
cuts its pure objective passion across the sky of your heart,
and on this conscious Tuesday you wonder what to do with the time
    that's left,
how to give up the self you know.
This one moment sitting in a chair, standing, walking, never ends,
has always tried to make you see that, hear that,
in the trivial daily decencies and secrets of your life.
This bit of time outweighs the clock,
this instant equals the great sigh of freedom
that lately calms you as if you possessed a different body.
No one knows what to do, and we all do it endlessly—
O salvation of not having died quite yet in each transit of breath.
Because we can't find terms for this maybe we will never
really live, but we get glimpses, hear it
in the simple abrupt hymn of leaves or a child's cry in the distance,

and the star that wakes my heart again
is a shield of beauty and I step forth without fear into the streaming flesh
     of time
and place my mouth tenderly against its mouth, that will devour us.
This is not one of those Japanese outbursts on the edge of death,
of clear identity, that dissolves death, in which a few images redefine the
     human,
it's too Western to be sane or wise or useful.
I'm alone. May the peace and stupidity of having no ideas
unveil what I know but cannot see or name.
Impossible—to be, where every face, gesture, phrase, shines
in a unique necessity of its own, which you cannot condemn.
Whoever sustained his arrogant certainties without fail
across your naked back with the sting of a whip
is dead. Now what? Who will you blame now? Fix your eyes on the wild
     sky,
which never thinks and is never the same, and ask it.

5 / IN THE INFINITIVE

IN THE INFINITIVE

1.
I'm often sitting on a stool in my calm living room
waiting for the message of appearances.

This is not a vocal stadium
for the arrival of voices, of excellences.

How many of you are waiting, too, for the stances
of reality to change, open like radium

Glowing inside a lead box, particle dances
twittering against the wild wall of appearances

Where we always find ourselves, where romances
break our hearts until we hear the hum

Of another life stumbling toward us
right up to our innocent faces?

I remember Robert Frost and George Herbert and John Donne
wrecking my heart with words, Hopkins, Dickinson

Walking right through me as if I were a room
open to the public, taking their chances

With me, and isn't it true, too, of you,
hasn't someone touched you with a voice

So tender you cried? Of course, every bodily cell says,
naturally, desire is a mire of unquenchable fire,

Lust, rust, crust, dust, must, trust,
or whatever rhymes make meaning poignant.

Take love, for example, do you know what it is,
is it little more than a sudden fizz

Of Christ knows what descending from the cross
to kiss your vacant lips and kill you, bless

Your fading bones with a kingdom of promises
no one will ever keep? Dark dark the question marks

Of this accidental life on this accidental earth,
and darker still some nights without faith, the dearth

Of purpose makes birch and magnolia in my yard shine
brighter, the sky takes on a tone

Of immeasurable value. So what? I light a cigar
out back under the trees and feel a childhood scar

On my elbow, in my mind, from falling off a bike, from trauma
after beautiful trauma, Look, I hear myself whisper to the trauma

Called myself, What the fuck do you want this time,
the solution to history's oldest crime,

A barbecue to distract you, a perfect bird to sing
"Darkness is approaching you on its infinite wing?"

No, the hot relentless comedy of your thoughts
will save you, depend on their insanely wrought

Roots to shoot up help or a massacre, fresh disaster.
Frost and Yeats can't do shit about this, listen to the plaster

Crumble until a crack shows and you have to call Jay
to fix it, or buy spackle and do it yourself. Why

Should this bother you? I can hear the street sincerely
echo whatever passes on it, a window slam, a weary

Child crying Ma! a bus wheezing its way up 20th Street,
a dog yelping, some asshole revving his motorcycle, sweet

Words floating right through the window glass
of my study, right through the clear stupidity

My face is because I pretend to be more than human,
as if no death will ever chew my eyes out. Soon

It will, right? soon I'll eat dinner, drink wine,
take my nonexistent dog out for a walk, feel him strain

On the leash and whine for his philistine life, too.
Lacan, would you agree? Probably not. But you

Don't know your ass from transference, I enjoy the heartless
theory you weave like armor, you should put your face

Low, lower, and taste the grass at your feet, you should wear
a copper top hat and watch it turn green, smear

Your hands with marmalade and lick it off in public,
but what I love most is a photo of Bernard Hinaut

Frozen, leaning over his handlebars, mouth open, stretched wide
rabid like a tiger's as he bears down, bent

On finishing first, his upper arms hard as rock.
And so, his grandeur makes Lacan sound like a quack,

Though I love the fact that he needed to dominate
all shrinks with his mystifying ideas, ruminate

Their worshiping brains into a pulp he could eat.
Even when we wake in the middle of the night to pee

It's with us—the tacit music of the spheres, the erratic
brain hearing itself make nonsense out of nothingness, the vatic

Aspirations, pleas, looninesses, coughs, and belches
of identity washing its hands before it loses

Itself again in sleep. Someone put this idiotic hammer in
my hands and I just held each nail of a word between

My thick poetic fingers and bonged each one
hard into the frail wall of a page, into the ruin

Of sense that supports nothing. Ok, I'll condense this prolegomena,
this intro to a loss I can't define—Hippolytos,

Stunned by the force of sex, of blindness to another's life,
Oedipus, bleeding from the sockets of his eyes—who's safe?

Or to put it another way—don't forget to lock the back door
each night or who knows what'll sneak in when you're asleep,

Stand over you in bed and watch you breathe, examine your mussed
    hair,
and, like a god in your dreams, silently weep.

2.
I could wake every morning happy, make toast, coffee,
thank God I have two hands and feet, but there's this idea:

Do we ever understand what we think? quoting Jung
in his book on Man's search for a soul, for a song

To pin down once and for all this life-and-death life
in plain speech, in ecstatic talk, in terms of belief

That don't wear out in a day. Even dumbfounded we love its insane
physical beauties—everywhere, everything kisses our lone

Bodies all over. I remember someone saying
"Nobody can save the snow," it's written on the first page

Of Canto XX in my "Purgatorio" where Dante mentions people
who pour from their eyes drop by drop the evil

That fills the entire world, I don't know where it came from
or why it's there, like "The natural thirst which is never quenched"

From the same Italian pen. The thing is, I recognize the storm
of desire behind those words, how often I've flinched

At the thought of resolving it. Wait a minute, I'm not serious
about anything anymore, am I, I'm not a delirious

Truth-seeker, an adolescent hounding identity
from one girl to the next? Maybe the soul is really

A garter belt and stockings dancing without a body
in front of my rapt face, mouth drooling moronically,

Maybe God is a tugboat pulling a luxury liner
out of port on its way to Japan or China.

How should I know? It's one of those aimless days
when I could say anything, when even the words of Marcus Aurelius,

The sanest man who ever tried to advise our poor souls,
make sense, or, in a bolder vein, Dogen's

Obvious contradictory "life does not obstruct death, and death
does not obstruct life," feels like an angel's breath

Pulsing on my cheek. How many times has breakfast
been enough, how many dinners have I eaten too fast

Because I wanted to reach the next thing, whatever it was,
be somewhere else, while the fish and potatoes

Rumbled and gave me heartburn? I'm stuck here, on this chair,
stool to be accurate, waiting for my head to clear,

grateful to see and speak;
I'd give you all my money if you'd take

A snapshot of yourself reading this
so I could see what you look like, bless

the image of yourself waiting for what will never come,
knowing that the chair you sit on and the room

Are merely experimental gifts. I love to touch things
but, like Simone Weil (she was never a girlfriend), says,

"Man's great affliction, which begins with infancy and accompanies
him till death, is that looking and eating are two different operations.

Eternal beatitude is a state where to look is to eat."
What a lunatic! I guess she forgot about meat

And all the other food, from bagels and lox to rich red wine.
It's understandable: she starved herself to death, to help striking workers,

But I don't want to screw myself like that, I'm not a loon
who needs to become a saint, I'd rather watch alligators

In the zoo tear flesh or bask like logs scarcely
visible above water, or imagine a bare young body

Wearing that ghostly garter belt, those stockings, resurrected
from the land of the dead. What I've always expected

From life is millions of dollars, endless great sex,
zero suffering, effortless motion like a stupid bird

gliding from point to point, and of course immortality, but the axe
of time is falling, dear silent friend, and I hear

Once you're dead that's it. Oh well, I'll rent
a violent movie, feed my illusory goldfish, strangle the cat

Next door that keeps shitting on my patio out back,
pissing on plants and chairs, squatting in the sun

As if my beautifully groomed yard were his, as if I weren't sufficiently
    racked
by passion and despair and needed to put up with his insouciant bullshit,

His cat's apathetic gaze. I used to be like him, able to nap for hours in
     the sun,
feeling the sky and air and breeze as one big tit,

In fact, that's much of what I did in Mexico for two years
before I moved back to America, had kids, became a doleful employee,

Slowly realized a plight that has no name, whose tears
remind me often I'm in it, no way out, softer

Inside, tainted with what Wittgenstein calls the "if-feeling."
There's that motherfucking cat again, posing on a rock

As if he owns the universe. It would be healing
to hold open a short thick rubber band and snap it around his neck.

3.
In these circumstances I can only think of shit,
that hated, inescapable stuff—you take your chances

Every day, eat junk, fresh vegetables, turkey, etc.,
that turns into this thing you shun as you would a murderer

Even though you produce it, it's necessary, you leave it everywhere,
in streets, woods, alleys, backyards, lawns, on underwear.

Once I had to go through it with my bare hands looking
for a gold cap I thought I swallowed that had slipped off a tooth.

I noticed it was gone at a restaurant, eating lunch, probing
with the tip of my tongue lettuce caught between molars. Shit's truth

Is its fibrous browns, unlike anything else we know,
its pungent rare stench, a kind of spirit perfume wafted from far below

The mind's need to discriminate. For two days I leaned over the bowl
after each dump and picked apart my own beloved foul

Faeces, commenting to myself on the sundry lumps and strings
and corn shards from last night's partying,

Squeezing it between my fingers to make sure my fake tooth
hadn't dropped out of my mouth. That afternoon, sitting in the booth

With a composer friend of mine, I was questioning him about music's
fortunate abstract power to explore the heart's

Secret core, that place inside us—oh, we know it's there—
where who we really are that others can't know waits to be known,

Cradled in benevolent hands, talked to in a voice
so rich with kindness death fades into mist and the air

Touches us like a blessing everywhere.
He didn't agree with me, he said you had to face

The absurd obstacle of hearing it first with no clear sense
that proves what you hear has meaning, then finally, of course,

You do it—write down notes. I told him music reminded me
of someone without a face, without that clear physical identity,

While words kept the human image alive, you always know
what someone's saying, what it means, you "recognize." There was snow

On the pavement when we left. I kept flicking at the stub
of my tooth as we slipped now and then walking to the parking lot,

Fat flakes swept down suddenly, popping on our tongues as we spoke.
Hey, I said, maybe music is like a snowfall inside the mind, a soul

Tossed into the world, instantly dissolving, renewing itself,
like time, and we are time, but can't make

Ourselves always feel it so we can live it so we can stop lamenting our
     brief
lives; maybe we should make falling snow a rule

We follow, winter or not, identify with the humiliated flakes,
so unassuming, speechless, frail, how can they not help but teach us.

4.
Pile boot atop chair atop wagon atop sunflowers atop insanity
atop the field he looked at day after day.

Evening would flip its thin black lid down over his eyes,
he'd try to sleep, couldn't, would kneel to nothingness,

stare out the window into the distance, will
into focus the end of it, invoke it like a white stone wall.

In the room they gave him in the asylum, something behind a wall
scratched for food, table creaked, faucet sang its bleak remorseful note.

The doctor told him cure was simply not dwelling on God or Love
or the impossibility of getting yellow to represent

The soul of wheat, blue the soul of the sky, was keeping his
mind on other things, which he always tried to, his mind on

Whether he would ever kiss a woman's breasts again
or feel himself effaced, inside her, so worry would flee once

And for all in the ecstatic instant inside, the infinite instant—
Reality for him now—who strove incessantly, blessed,

As the scourge of The Greater Mind subsumed him, used him,
replaced him with its law that makes all into a facsimile of Being—

Because It once made whatever is then let it be, & could only
let it remain in sin for a while, otherwise World

Would end forever—this wild skill of existence a force beyond the
        human he
submitted to, prayed to, vessel of God's ruinous decree

To take all back to beginnings, endings. I simply felt the need
that day to visit the museum, stopped in front of his painting

Stricken by its exalted melancholy grays greens blues. They had
rearranged the Impressionists and Post Impressionists,

So many I had looked at countless times were hung in new bright places,
the lighting completely redone. The day he painted *Rain*

How could he have made the falling rain fall with such life
it still falls on the motionless canvas, and as I stood

There fell inside me, and still falls, drenching boot chair wagon,
all eaten into infinity by the God-thing (pitiful man to need it),

How made the crooked sterile field, its three stone walls, so kindly askew,
trees, two shacks, the shorn awful unending distance,

Who tore himself apart to be in, to become—I say he saw Death,
painting it himself out there beyond actual space, without hands, say too

Where God, where you, are the same, whatever you do
God does, creation and created simultaneous grievous oracular fire,
    signed Vincent.

6 / OBLIVION

When these elements vanish,

they don't say 'I' vanish.

—DOGEN

a child's arms opening (it's strapped in a stroller, zipped into a snowsuit), mine flung out too in spontaneous embrace as we pass, strangers ages apart on the crowded Christmas street rapt in identity, "the blight man was born for"? a despair warns us, as we pass, the packed decorated store windows winking at us, the few dead I knew, relatives, friends, still speak to me as if they needed something, food? an idea? hope? to let me know the chaos of death, to teach me disappearance in silence, we never want to be there, it's the hell we're in now because we never want to be there, each of us a shred of memory about to evaporate in someone's mind, remember me, please, or else how can I be? where can I be? "When I'm dead I won't have anything" my mother said, meaning I won't have consciousness, and we accept it all, you, I, look, look around you, think, try, retreat, touch whatever is near, undergo yourself like this, who can't keep anything, one story to cling to might stop it, the one about, no doubt you'll tell it, but now obsession with the dead and afterlife, like static, code, the night sky's indecipherable face, its clots, washes, yesterday, tomorrow, now, do we become stars? would that console us? no knowledge, no one to hear or touch in the middle of the night, no sweet familiar breath, this voice urging itself to forget explanation, remembering, forgetting, the sociomystical core of its being, for others, for yourself, for God, that indecipherable word, whose breath still mists a window, still justifies the self's quest to unveil itself beyond itself into a full fierce communion of truth, face looking out, face looking back at me, ". . . for love is exultant when it unites equals but it is triumphant when it makes that which was unequal equal in love, every point of departure in time is . . . accidental, an occasion, a vanishing moment, the teacher himself is no more than this, who philosophizes with equal absoluteness everywhere, and the thinker without a paradox is like a lover without feeling, the supreme paradox of all thought is the attempt to discover something that thought cannot think, this passion is at bottom present in all thinking, even in the thinking of the individual in so far as in thinking he participates in something transcending himself," oblivion the core, everywhere, nowhere, the final invisible basis, images sketched in a void, delicate pencil lines forming— a street, a man prostrate on his back, arms out, head lolled over, a mutt sniffing the man's neck under his chin, some witnesses standing to one side of the body, above his faceless face lapsed away from the spectators a shape persists like the breath of a miscreated god, like a burst of exhaust in cold, a ghostly residue belonging to a different, fuller story that hovers the way thought will when it appears, fades to a fragment of memory, of blood—once in a dream I saw my life take shape, a complete story whose meaning is clearly known, a real story about real people, real things, not like this, and when I woke everything—bed sheets, blankets, rugs, chairs, walls, the sky—glowed like myth because the gods were alive and shed upon the earthly world their impossible immortal glory

•

O angel with black wings, on cellar stairs leading up out of the darkness into the light, so-called, the light, O waking dream of one, sleep dream of another, no place to start, no place to end, no place anywhere in these fables of ourselves, she told me in the elevator rising to her office when she and her husband were making love she would see black wings, eyes closed, she felt heavy, a slender woman, her husband said he felt light, and I saw myself climbing a flight of stairs, up from the cellar, and on each step a man, some well dressed, some in work clothes, at attention, like a series of guards hired to watch me as I ascended toward the so-called light, light of oblivion, truth, whatever name we reach for, up up until having assessed each one in a mild panic of apprehension I reached the door into probably a kitchen where one was waiting, dressed in an elegant blue double-breasted suit, handmade from the cut of the lapels and buttonholes, there, he looked straight into my eyes and grabbed me by the neck, unzipped my pants, somebody else must have held me, tore off my shorts, pulled out a switchblade, razor sharp, I could see how the light smoldered along its edge, reached down and took both my testicles in his right hand, hard, and swept the blade across the scrotum at the top by the asshole at the root of the penis and swooped both balls off whoosh and thrust them up to my face in his bloody hand, I roared and lunged and battered his face to a red mess, then woke early, before dawn, wobbled out of bed, the dream preceding that one vanished, born again and again and again at the cost of castration, now the wings of the angel make sense, and the husband's nearly weightless pleasure, because she told me, too, just as we reached her floor, she had several other fantasies whirling around inside while they did it, black wings might represent some unrecognized god making itself known, some resistance of the flesh to a meaning, a suffering bound up with being entered, the resurrected absence-of-all-without-loss—to rise into the light and the death that waits for us, its kind bleak shining eyes like yours when you were a child and looked down and noticed a pretty stone or a dead bug and took it home and saved it

•

desiring, having, if we could tell the difference between them death wouldn't matter anymore, even suicide would be good, a remedial flight from the life the suicide could not live, as an undoing, a failed transcendence, Sidney Goodman's *A Man's Arm* is a painting of desiring, of having, mute contradiction, the right side of the body hidden behind a wall, the upper left part of the chest and the entire left arm thrust out, hand making a fist, arm turned forward, inner arm facing us, all in a horizontal red and black box of space behind the arm, a flat blank surface below it, all framed by grayish washes, browns, the arm trapped in hellish immobility, the heart side isolated, no head, no other image, the rest of the body gone behind the windowlike shape containing the arm, which can't look out, see anything, of course, but stays there fixed in place by the person who's invisible, this lone limb pleads, refuses, strips itself, speaks of the inarticulate fated life in the flesh it is, black smeared where a chunk of head might be, behind the frame, a doorframe? black smeared about the wrist and fist like a cloud, a battle of inner gods, selfhood seeking a self, gesture suggesting one of those gently crescent-shaped Japanese sword blades I saw in a Washington museum, without hilts, five of them, narrow mirrors, resting in wooden cradles, full white artificial light, breath prints, memory, result of ancient fire, pale silhouettes emanating from the steel, the upturned sharp edge imperceptible as the air of their glass cases

•

103

I was nobody, 19, wandering Greenwich Village, in an elevator with Ginsberg going to a party, sitting in a strange apartment, facing an empty chair when the door flies open and Keruoac bounds across the room, jumps into the chair in front of me, wiggles his fat face, leers, "Got any questions? I got the answers!"—the intro to a meditative text? a secret voice infected with The Truth? reaching for a red flower? for notes on the artless art? on ignorance and essence? a phone rings on the street, twenty or thirty times, we've all heard it, I'm passing one of those aluminum phone booths and the bell is ringing, keeps ringing, like the loneliness I feel, the emptiness, I'm half a block away, I hear it, it must be someone I know, I think, it must be someone I would recognize, holding the receiver to her ear, hearing me, wanting me, sitting in a window overlooking the street, waiting for someone's despair to lift the receiver, not conscious yet of the depths where intolerable self waits for the final deprivation to reveal itself, to fuse you to it, known soul to unknown soul, once when Jeff and I waited for a bus on Broad Street one of those phones rang and rang until I picked it up, a woman's voice wanted to know what I liked, if I liked having it taken in all the way up to the balls, the tongue prodding it, slowly, then hard against the shaft up to the tip until it's cupped and savored by the lips, if I liked all of it, all, then the questions again, the exciting shifts of detail, her blank, fakely ecstatic voice, like a bad actor's, then "You don't really like it," when I hesitated to respond, I wanted to meet her, spend time, was terrified, I wanted to forget the salesmanship, the artificial eagerness in her tone, the fraction of sincerity, I could see us one late winter afternoon in her apartment, she acting like a girl on her first date being dirty, me hearing the high indifference of my fears squawk chitchat while all I wanted was—you know . . . then the image of her accomplice stepping out of a closet, poised over us naked in bed, beating the shit out of me with a baseball bat, laughing, the whole thing flaying me, wrecking me, opening bad bad depths beneath depths of a hell of questions, nausea, a list of nameless terrors, qualms, boundaries, quandaries, notes heard by some anonymous eerie ear, not mine, not music yet, not sense, no last redemptive music beginning it, ending it, no method memory knows

•

"In their suffering is there hope"—nothing could terrify, be more tragic than what I dreamed last night—my younger daughter, Margot, age 3, holding a doll, standing beside me in Mexico, perhaps, on a high balcony overlooking a plaza, the bright dry sun gilding her face, eyes luminous, her stiff blue cotton dress riffling when the wind rises, girl frozen on that spot in tiny shiny red leather shoes, a few feet back from the rail, taking in the scenery, which is probably a white village with a church on the plaza (a faded movie set?), bare stores, a few streets feeding into the plaza, stucco houses, simple and small, on the edge of desert, people strolling or walking, dogs, parked cars, bicycles, thick deep green trees, not many, jutting out of the sand on the edge of the streets, no, out of the springwater clear air, then the terrible thing happens in a detailed rush: her doll leaps out of her arms and flies away between lower and upper bars of the iron railing and falls and she reaches to keep it and keeps reaching to keep it and has no idea where she is as she reaches through the bars into the distance and follows the doll down ten storeys, ten slow long storeys, I don't lift a finger, I remember deciding not to move, I just don't move—so afraid of losing her, or anything, that movement is impossible—a punishment so far beyond the crime no crime remains, only punishment, like Dante's sickening symbol of the man-sized lizard and the man standing facing each other in Hell, the creature's forelegs lifted high, like arms, pressing against the man's raised arms, each pair of limbs touching the entire length, as if an invisible mirror between them functions like clear glass but could still reflect, fuse, and transform the creature and the man into each other, into a single organism, slow, excruciatingly slow, according to the poet, each inch of the creature and the human being at one point truly unified until an excruciated, third, new brute is formed, but of course it was the man who suffered infinitely through eternity, the man-tall lizard was the force that sucked him in, gripped, consumed, recast his identity inside that ravishing body of torment that the man, still fully conscious of himself throughout the process, would inhabit forever as himself as alien, and I sobbed as only a person can, chest and belly spasmodically awry, mouth ripped open, in tatters, quivering, a grief howled through me— back now in the dream of my falling daughter—a passion from nowhere, no one, hailstorm, no meaning, no interpretation to serve as salvation, only that fragile straw of a line about suffering and hope at the beginning of this, only that tenuous straw of a voice

•

through William Carlos Williams I heard from the dead, dead what? dead who? through the one unnameable forger of forms, they squealed a little, they were happy, he was a sort of leader in the no heaven no hell courage of after, before it we're terrified, after it's all pure courage because we know, not anything special, voices, choral yet each one rapid and clear, somehow in unison uttering differences, on the afterlife as a continual inner voice without definite emphasis or identity, each point made and abandoned, afterlife as voice, where one becomes the voice of one's self fully, finally the billions of dead all singing and talking at once, and yet if you are one of them, which I was momentarily, you can pick one to listen to then let it fade, it isn't a din or threatening chaos, merely a degree of communion unheard-of, unknown, impossible where other acts, here in this ordinary life, have so much meaning, ". . . the pleasure, for me, is in speaking, as if words enclosed the secret in myself that lasts after death," sang dear friend Michael Ryan in his rigorous chaste tongue, or ". . . deport yourself naturally like moonbeams flooding into a leaky cottage," time, time, and the ages of us, "I am a wholeness I'll never know. Maybe that's the best," O beautiful Carruth, but it was the Doctor from New Jersey who began my twisted song as we finished giving ourselves in bed and slept, his fresh breakings of the soil of form athwart my eyes, as if something will always grow, which he believed, as long as one is honest, a breaking of the mind across form, or its opposite, so many opposites in his work, "Forget poetry," he says, and you could say he wrote already dead, the floor of his mind strewn with remnants of an ancient joyous culture, he redefined the tragic with a glance at the empty sky, with loving disdain, at "the eyes of women," rotted here in the wet inner flesh of love, "upon me," he would say, or "the stillness of this squalid corner," it could be anything anywhere, his mind seized and splintered out of itself, into itself, torn always like a laughing saint, hard cock and a quick mind, too quick for language itself, but we want to know about death, above all, though it doesn't exist, Williams told me in the dream, I was waking from sleep after love, in both worlds, when I heard him say it, no death, imageless, fear purified by fear, "nothing disliked or longed for," a kingdom of the voice with words lying idle that speak of who we are again again again until we break into each other in innocent faith "where other fathoms other . . . where water speaks of water," listen, talk to me, say anything, what is this place? oh yes, I remember, Williams calls it East CooCoo

•

about the woman who told me her lover's trick—he liked to hold a little rectangular cosmetic mirror in one hand while they fucked, manouver it close to their genitals and look back into it to watch his cock garage itself, withdraw, lips folding inward outward around it all aglistened, it was like a rearview mirror she said, a teaching instrument, but primarily it turned their act into a past icon that stayed alive, a living snapshot that moved, a screen, a transient film, a device for leaping outside one's life beyond death, of possessing and abandoning, and then, of course, of obliterating one zone of experience, one flesh and blood zone, uplifting it into a paradise of pure capture, of imagery without substance, something like what a believable definition of heaven might be if only the mirror did not need a world outside itself to fill it but continued to reflect, from inside itself, the images of a world, like forgetting one's body, face, affections, unintelligible desires, memories, hopes, regrets, interrupted glimpses of another self, unpredictably born over the years, like transforming it all into a thing separate from itself, a thing with genitals while the genitals by themselves did what they did together, two nonexistent identities, two godlike nobodies nothing but powers surging toward . . . ? a mirror facing a mirror? "Will life become clear to us and we unable to say what our sense of it is?" I guess the thinker wrote it to give faith, or to make me worry

•

and yet Homer's dream descriptions always give the circumstances before the dream, the dream image moving toward the sleeper, standing above the sleeper's head, then the speech of the dream image, then aftermath, all's outside, the populated cosmos gives itself to the dreamer, all inner life portrayed outside, like the reader's freedom to enter the text as anyone, as the speaking ghost itself, ideal, redeemed, uttered into the false immortal air of civilized memory . . . so this is oblivion—"The subject is not something given, it is something added and invented and projected behind what there is. The subject is the fiction that many similar states in us are the effect of one substratum . . . the fundamental false observation that I believe it is I who do something, suffer something, have something, have a 'quality,'"—but the dead, who were they? are they? where? if we could only speak but we never speak, never have said one word that doesn't lead to the next, a mist of uncertainty, nevertheless go on, Sunday, it was, after the fire that drove her from her apartment, a sick old woman living by the sea, back with her son and his wife after the fire, waiting to go back home, dreaming about dead friends, telling her son, sitting up in bed, singing her hopeful song, "Are you listening!" she snapped, sitting bent on the edge of the bed, pushing herself up on skinny arms, looking down, into herself, into the blanket, into the floor, dried irises shrunk among roses carnations ferns curving out of a vase by the bed on the high dresser, her son sitting in a rocker, watching, listening, old mother on the edge of oblivion, I have to tell the story I heard rocking in front of her, are you listening? I, she said, visiting my mother's sister, Anna, I was just a little tot, we'd walk all the way across town from West Philadelphia to Girard Avenue to visit Anna and her husband, they had money, compared to us, and we'd sit all afternoon nibbling, the four of us, on one measly can of salmon, they were so cheap! then afterwards they didn't even offer to drive us home, we didn't have a car of course, so we'd walk back all that way, I remember being tired and I remember my father would play a game with me by taking my hand, him on one side, my mother on the other, they'd take my hands and he'd say, "Close your eyes, go to sleep," and they'd walk me home that way with my eyes closed telling me when a curb was coming, when to step over a hole, my father would say now and then in this strong gentle voice, "Go to sleep, go to sleep," it was such a long walk, and I'd walk in the darkness that way until we got home, my eyes closed all the way, funny, I dreamed last night about all my dead friends, Bea, Bernie, all of them, then I remembered this, it was sweet to walk home in the dark like that, I think they took me to my aunt's house because I was fun, I know my brother never went, oh yes, there was always talk, music, food at our house, my mother would scrub the porch steps and the porch, the old days, I was happy, I was bad but happy, my father had the most beautiful handwriting, and a soft voice

•

believe believe believe, red, yellow, and blue soulbird hovering above Cézanne's skull on a mantel, who sings? what sings? sometimes it seems everyone sings, everything sings, happy about something without know-ing, stricken by something without caring, oh living helpless things, readers, "so like myself, indeed, so brotherly," what of another's torment, what of ours? seduction, annihilating lesson, fate, benign indifference, unattainable self, who who who, nothing between who and who, text, think of the earth, think of the unquestioning earth, dark mirror that takes us into itself, oh helpless living things, dwelt nowhere, believe believe believe but in what in who, our lack of faith so agonizing we can barely breathe without feeling the rasp of absence in our throats, barely attain a sense of the miracle, barely balance ourselves between one moment and the next, "here is the place, here the way unfolds," even the morphine drip? even the morphine drip, even her cold white bony face? even her cold white face, "no" when we tried to feed her a slice of orange at the end, "no no no" when we kissed her brow, "no no" to a sip of water, "no" to the room "no no no" to a bit of cake, "no" to the light, to the nurse, "no no" to a word of hope, "no no no no," it was when she slipped com-pletely into silence that the silence dawned and became a different silence in the midst of silence, it was when I felt something like a clean white shirt drop across my shoulders that forever, that's the word, forever forever forever, better than believe unless they're bought together into, unless you understand that belief is the weight of the calcium ash and the thudding of bone chunks inside the spun bronze urn, believe that her long ears and the stately bent nose and the sweet wet bulgy eyes and feet that still looked like a thirty-year-old's, believe they were ash and are ash and are not ash and were not ash, "so if I dreame I have you, I have you," how can I say it? "where other fathoms other," to give you it as the universe is given, like Perseus who went down into death to cut off the head of fear, but do we understand? do we know how? it was very quiet in the fifth-floor hall, nurses were doing chores, taking notes, ducking into rooms, answering phones, standing and chatting, when I came in that morning the irises still looked fresh, stiff, their throats, scarred yellow and white, yawned, the petals curled back in an ecstatic retreat from the bravery of their own forms, the yellow button-shaped bunch mixed with the irises were also bright and firm, fanning out among the irises, their hue echoing that other, similar yellow streaked inside the irises, words have no right to be here in that room, in memory, the flowers are simpler things, my mother's drained face, waiting for nothing, expecting nothing, the skinny plastic tube snaked into her arm, you could say, was invented to give her back to a state of nature, to give us, humans, on the verge of death, since nature is what it is and does not need our help, since we have lost it in ourselves and need . . . well, that doesn't matter . . . the flowers were the silence she had come to in her life, you could say her eyelids drawn over her eyes glowed like the petals of those flowers, pale purplish oily gray, like a winter sky, not like those flowers, the eyeball itself blind behind the motionless lid, those flowers in my mind punish me still, their trite incomparable beauty! how shamelessly they gave themselves, no matter what was happening, how like a gift of grace, even when I leaned down to press my face against her cheek their faces hovered above the bed table, flared, "where other fathoms other," nothing diminishes their insult, nothing helps me to fathom how they got there, could exist, could come to be at all, the small plastic cup, comb, lipstick, paper slippers, digital TV, oxygen stored by her head inside the wall, the waning daylight window, chocolates, none eaten, the commode inches away that took all her strength, all of it, just to sit up and wrench herself out of bed to reach it and be eased down by someone else's hands to pee, "here is the place, here the way unfolds," the sheet tucked neatly across her chest, arms under it, like swaddling, her straight gray hair cut short pinned back as always at the temple with a child's barrette, the guileless store-bought bouquet, still thrusting, opening, offering

•

ghost figures roam the area, disc of the thin white moon, obstacle, writing itself and all the terms and forms, what is it? care? bullshit? killing time? something in us needs words, something in us is words, talk to me, hold me, momentary salvation, what works between us, what brings us back to each other in ourselves, ghost figures roam the area, smooth as a cloud-less sky, not anywhere, where death is, where it belongs, ghost figures roam . . . one night in Peru, Vermont, a bunch of us, in August, cooked out on the edge of a huge field, waiting for the lunar eclipse, ghost fig-ures roaming the field, eating, talking, watching, yearning into the moist grass our hands and faces, tasting the grass, passing each other in the dark, walking out into it alone to the field's edge where trees went on forever, returning to a blanket where a few sat not quite seeing each other, hands grazing hands, eyes barcly alive to eyes, smelling the barbecue charcoals waft by, as the crisp moon inched across, it was as if we had dematerial-ized by half but had lost nothing of ourselves, as if daylight had been an unrecognized obstacle blinding us to the intimacy we had always desired and could only find like this, the word communion seems appropriate, objects looked graver, symbolically reborn into some aura of pristine holy meaning, we had entered a state latent but unrealized because we had given ourselves so many reasons, until this accident of nature, this event that became a pretext for something, not the old idea of epiphany, but something else, ghost figures roam the area, as if the line between life and death evaporated, just people in the place, friends, just the courage of good feeling, so the night of the eclipse this long gray cloud spuming out of its top clung to the moon like a feathered crown, shining, wavering, a wall of trees on three sides blackly stayed, silence, uncanny peace rose between us, which was, I am now sure, the fellowship of ghost figures, not us, and yet us, themselves manifesting their wish to let us know what was possible but an ordeal to sustain, to experience believably at all . . .

soon the bottom of the sky radiated a weird bluish steely hue upward, igniting the foaming crown, piercing it, making it vibrate with sanctified light, the treetops shone, off and on, black clarities, ominously serrated profiles, then sank back into the lesser dark of the sky, O broken bird, the phrase won't go away, last night it stayed with me until I slept, introductory, beckoning, flutelike, a troubling supplication to begin, what? I know what it was, the voice in us whispering its loving motherly phrases to quell fear, that whole night outside in the field waiting for the moon to disappear was like being held in compassionate hands, safe, a broken bird in unknown pitying hands, O broken bird of our life, that night in the transcendental field—at one point the sky gave off enough light to see by, made everyone, everything, look transparent, auraed, substantial but not opaque, draped in white patina, we were ghost figures living in a world released from the difference between life and death, no longer plagued by mortality, no longer conscious of the impossibility of resolving the breach between life and death, we danced without a particular pattern of steps, whatever we did had the grace of clouds immersed in their own purposeless transfigurations, something, nothing, anything, we sat, stood, walked, ran, leaned on each other, dropped down on the grass, rambled into the trees to smell them, whisper to them, embrace them, it was nothing much, no more in a way than that sad confession we all probably have made, that takes many forms—"When I saw any external object, my consciousness that I was seeing it would remain between me and it, enclosing it in a slender, incorporeal outline which prevented me from ever coming directly in contact with the material form: for it would volatilize itself in some way before I could touch it, just as an incandescent body which is moved towards something wet never actually touches moisture, since it is always preceded, itself, by a zone of evaporation."—a week ago a dream came, in a series of dreams, about a "Zen Clock," which appeared in the dream, amazingly part of me, maybe I should say *on* me, I was wearing a pale coat, vestment, gown or robe, and painted on the front from chin to ankle in black was a perfect clock with a pure white face, it had only one hand, pointing straight down to the 6, a black arrow hand, tip grazing the hem, brushing my feet, I awoke the moment I saw the clock, "who, when, where," all three were one in the dream, like actual people, time was not when but where I was, standing at any given moment, where pain, faith and salvation would have been absurdities of conceptual desperation, I . . . then, without warning, the disc of the shadow of the sun gnawed at the left side of the moon, bit into it, absorbed it by degrees until a crude glow thorned its rim—"disciple" means to discover God as human consciousness recovering its source in nature, in the faith that looks through death, disciple means the discipline of humiliation by the real—then, then the moon, that had dwindled into a halo of lost light, began to slip back into sight, until it was whole again, miraculously there, no one spoke, we stood there, mortal without thought, untold stories of ourselves, I

ILLINOIS POETRY SERIES
Laurence Lieberman, Editor

History Is Your Own Heartbeat
Michael S. Harper (1971)

The Foreclosure
Richard Emil Braun (1972)

The Scrawny Sonnets and Other Narratives
Robert Bagg (1973)

The Creation Frame
Phyllis Thompson (1973)

To All Appearances: Poems New and Selected
Josephine Miles (1974)

The Black Hawk Songs
Michael Borich (1975)

Nightmare Begins Responsibility
Michael S. Harper (1975)

The Wichita Poems
Michael Van Walleghen (1975)

Images of Kin: New and Selected Poems
Michael S. Harper (1977)

Poems of the Two Worlds
Frederick Morgan (1977)

Cumberland Station
Dave Smith (1977)

Tracking
Virginia R. Terris (1977)

Riversongs
Michael Anania (1978)

On Earth as It Is
Dan Masterson (1978)

Coming to Terms
Josephine Miles (1979)

Death Mother and Other Poems
Frederick Morgan (1979)

Goshawk, Antelope
Dave Smith (1979)

Local Men
James Whitehead (1979)

Searching the Drowned Man
Sydney Lea (1980)

With Akhmatova at the Black Gates
Stephen Berg (1981)

Dream Flights
Dave Smith (1981)

More Trouble with the Obvious
Michael Van Walleghen (1981)

The American Book of the Dead
Jim Barnes (1982)

The Floating Candles
Sydney Lea (1982)

Northbook
Frederick Morgan (1982)

Collected Poems, 1930–83
Josephine Miles (1983)

The River Painter
Emily Grosholz (1984)

Healing Song for the Inner Ear
Michael S. Harper (1984)

The Passion of the Right-Angled Man
T. R. Hummer (1984)

Dear John, Dear Coltrane
Michael S. Harper (1985)

Poems from the Sangamon
John Knoepfle (1985)

In It
Stephen Berg (1986)

The Ghosts of Who We Were
Phyllis Thompson (1986)

Moon in a Mason Jar
Robert Wrigley (1986)

Lower-Class Heresy
T. R. Hummer (1987)

Poems: New and Selected
Frederick Morgan (1987)

Furnace Harbor: A Rhapsody of the
North Country
Philip D. Church (1988)

Bad Girl, with Hawk
Nance Van Winckel (1988)

Blue Tango
Michael Van Walleghen (1989)

Eden
Dennis Schmitz (1989)

Waiting for Poppa at the Smithtown Diner
Peter Serchuk (1990)

Great Blue
Brendan Galvin (1990)

What My Father Believed
Robert Wrigley (1991)

Something Grazes Our Hair
S. J. Marks (1991)

Walking the Blind Dog
G. E. Murray (1992)

The Sawdust War
Jim Barnes (1992)

The God of Indeterminacy
Sandra McPherson (1993)

Off-Season at the Edge of the World
Debora Greger (1994)

Counting the Black Angels
Len Roberts (1994)

Oblivion
Stephen Berg (1995)

To Us, All Flowers Are Roses
Lorna Goodison (1995)

Honorable Amendments
Michael S. Harper (1995)

Points of Departure
Miller Williams (1995)

NATIONAL POETRY SERIES

Eroding Witness
Nathaniel Mackey (1985)
Selected by Michael Harper

Palladium
Alice Fulton (1986)
Selected by Mark Strand

Cities in Motion
Sylvia Moss (1987)
Selected by Derek Walcott

The Hand of God and a Few
Bright Flowers
William Olsen (1988)
Selected by David Wagoner

The Great Bird of Love
Paul Zimmer (1989)
Selected by William Stafford

Stubborn
Roland Flint (1990)
Selected by Dave Smith

The Surface
Laura Mullen (1991)
Selected by C. K. Williams

The Dig
Lynn Emanuel (1992)
Selected by Gerald Stern

My Alexandria
Mark Doty (1993)
Selected by Philip Levine

The High Road to Taos
Martin Edmunds (1994)
Selected by Donald Hall

Theater of Animals
Samn Stockwell (1995)
Selected by Louise Glück

OTHER POETRY VOLUMES

Local Men and *Domains*
James Whitehead (1987)

Her Soul beneath the Bone: Women's Poetry
on Breast Cancer
Edited by Leatrice Lifshitz (1988)

Days from a Dream Almanac
Dennis Tedlock (1990)

Working Classics: Poems on Industrial Life
Edited by Peter Oresick and Nicholas Coles
(1990)

Hummers, Knucklers, and Slow Curves:
Contemporary Baseball Poems
Edited by Don Johnson (1991)

The Double Reckoning of Christopher
Columbus
Barbara Helfgott Hyett (1992)

Selected Poems
Jean Garrigue (1992)

New and Selected Poems, 1962–92
Laurence Lieberman (1993)

The Dig and *Hotel Fiesta*
Lynn Emanuel (1994)

For a Living: The Poetry of Work
Edited by Nicholas Coles and Peter Oresick
(1995)